THE  HAWAIIANS

An Island People

BY

HELEN GAY PRATT

Drawings by Rosamond S. Morgan
and Juliette May Fraser

CHARLES E. TUTTLE COMPANY
Rutland, Vermont & Tokyo, Japan

*Published by the Charles E. Tuttle Company, Inc.
of Rutland, Vermont & Tokyo, Japan
with editorial offices at
153 Milk Street, Boston, MA 02109*

*Copyright in Japan, 1963, by Charles E. Tuttle Co., Inc.
All rights reserved.*

International Standard Book No. 0-8048-1709-X

Reprinted 1996

PRINTED IN THE UNITED STATES

THE HAWAIIANS

An Island People

SOME HAWAIIAN FISH

Introduction

People who live self-sufficient lives in small, isolated islands have to adapt themselves to a restricted environment. Their problems are different from those faced by the early inhabitants of continents. The way in which they meet their problems is a part of man's struggle to maintain himself—a significant, though usually a neglected, part.

Hawaii has been chosen as the scene for the story of the adaptations made by an island people because the Hawaiian Islands are the only islands which are now an integral part of the United States. Many descendants of the people whose life is described here live today in the Islands. They are American citizens; they live in American communities. The old life described in this book disappeared long ago, but something of its heritage has, in Hawaii, become the heritage of all who live there today.

Children interested in primitive life will find much to interest them in life in old Hawaii, although that life was not primitive, in the strict sense of the word. It was primitive in that the Hawaiians had at their disposal the materials of primitive man—wood, stone, bone and shell. The use the Hawaiians made of these

materials was far from primitive, and the social organization of the Hawaiian people was advanced.

No one has ever known the Islands as intimately as the ancient Hawaiians knew them. No one has ever described the beautiful islands of Hawaii more poetically than the Hawaiian people themselves, in their old songs. Some of these have been quoted in this book, to give the readers, wherever they live, something of the appreciation of the island setting which the Polynesian ancestors possessed.

People who live in Hawaii, or visitors to the Islands, need only to raise their eyes to see:

> "Hawaii-with-the-green-back
> A land that was found in the ocean,
> That was thrown up from the sea,
> From the very depths of Kanaloa."

For the observer today, as well as for some ancient singer:

> "Makapuu climbs to the sky . . .
> While Ocean pounds and breaks at its base . . .
> The sea, the home of the gods."

And:

> "Kaena Point flies on its way
> Like a sea bird in fair weather;
> Like the wings of a swooping gull
> Are the cliffs of Nenelea;
> Like the lash of the sea bird's wings
> Is the curl of the breaking wave
> In the channel of Ieie."

The natural setting remains, with its surf, its cliffs, its pounding seas, its hanging skies, its mountains, its valleys.

The Hawaiian people did more than adapt themselves to a restricted natural environment. They knew and loved the beauty of their island home. Even the few snatches of Hawaiian poetry quoted in this book may bring the reader a real gift from the people of old Hawaii.

H. G. P.

Honolulu

Contents

xi

Illustrations

xiii

THE HAWAIIANS

An Island People

CHAPTER ONE

The Hawaiian People

LONG, LONG AGO, a few men were traveling on a little ship in a great ocean. Perhaps their ship had been blown far by a storm. They did not know where they were. One day they saw land! Perhaps this land had water for the thirsty travelers! Perhaps it had food for the hungry travelers!

The men paddled the ship over the last few miles. They came to the shore. They landed. The land they had found was Hawaii. They were the first men to step upon the shores of Hawaii.

Old Hawaiian songs say that the leader of these travelers was named Hawaii-loa. He gave his name to the largest island. He stayed in Hawaii.

Later, the story says, he returned to his old home for his wife and children. Many people went with him to Hawaii when he went back there with his family.

We do not know whether there ever was a real person named Hawaii-loa. We do know that long

3

ago people who came from the south found the islands of Hawaii, and stayed there to live.

The people who found Hawaii were island people. Their island homes were in a great ocean—the Pacific. They were the Polynesians. The Polynesians traveled far over the great ocean around their islands. They found and settled many islands. That is why their island homes are known as *Polynesia*. The name comes from two Greek words. One of them means *many*, the other means *island*.

The Polynesians who moved to Hawaii became Hawaiians. Most of the Hawaiians were tall and strong. Nearly all of them had brown eyes and black hair. Their teeth were strong and good. They spent most of their time out of doors, and wore little clothing. Their brown bodies were deeply tanned by the warm sunshine of their island home.

All the Hawaiians could swim and dive very well. They greatly enjoyed surfing. When the surf was not high enough, they called for a great surf, saying:

> "Arise, arise, ye great surfs . . .
> The powerful curling waves . . .
> Well up, long raging surf."

The Hawaiians enjoyed active sports and games. They liked to box. They liked to race. Once a year, all work was stopped for a time. All the people took

HAWAII IS DISCOVERED

part in games and sports. The season of games and sports was called the *Makahiki*.

Hawaiian chiefs were strong and powerful. The people told many stories about the things chiefs could do. A favorite story, told about several different chiefs, says:

"Our chief threw his spear from the seashore right through the mountain ridge far away. There is the hole in the mountain made by our chief's spear." One such hole is in the ridge behind Kaaawa on Oahu. Another is behind Anahola on Kauai.

Hawaiian men enjoyed hard games and sports. Once, long after other people had found Hawaii, a stranger asked, "Why do you work so hard, running and racing? Why don't you work harder in your fields instead?" The men answered, "We work hard enough in our fields to get food for our families and our guests. Why should we work harder to get more? We do not need it. We work because we have to. We run and race because we like to."

The Hawaiians knew their islands. They knew the seas which surrounded their islands. They loved their beautiful island home. This book tells you some of the things the Hawaiians knew about their islands. It tells you something about how the Hawaiians lived long ago.

CHAPTER TWO

Islands and Outline Maps

ON PAGE 9 is a picture of Rabbit Island. All around this island you see water. An *island* is a body of land entirely surrounded by water. Some islands are very small, like this one. Some are much larger.

All islands are smaller than continents. *Continents* are the largest bodies of land in the world. If you were in the middle of even the smallest continent, it would take you many days to walk to the ocean. If you were in the middle of any island in the sea, you could reach the sea in a much shorter time.

Rabbit Island is in the Pacific Ocean. *Oceans* are the largest bodies of water in the world. The Pacific Ocean is the largest ocean. Pacific island people live on small bodies of land, surrounded by the waters of the largest ocean.

The edge of any land which touches the ocean is called the *seashore* or *seacoast*, or, as we often say, the *shore*, or *coast*. You cannot see the whole shore or coast of this little island in the picture.

We can make a drawing which shows the whole coast or shore of Rabbit Island. This kind of drawing is an *outline map*. Here is an outline map of this island.

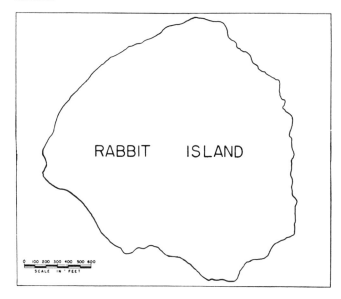

RABBIT   ISLAND

0 100 200 300 400 500 600
SCALE IN ' FEET

The outline map shows the shape of the whole island. The coast is not smooth. In some places, the ocean seems to go into the land. We say it *indents* the land. A place where the ocean indents the land is called a *bay* or *harbor*.

RABBIT ISLAND

Bays and harbors are useful. They are the safest places for ships and boats. If the shore of the bay is sandy, it is easy to take small boats and canoes to the shore.

The outline map shows where the bay is. It also shows the size of the island. In the corner of the map is a scale. It tells you how many feet on the island are represented by an inch on the map. If you measure the map, and use the scale, you can find out how wide the island is. You can find out how long the island is.

This island is very small, but we could not show its whole coast in a picture. If it were larger, we could show even less of it in a picture. We use outline maps instead of pictures to show the shapes and sizes of islands.

On page 11 is an outline map of the Hawaiian Islands. The map tells you the name of each of the eight islands.

The map shows you which island is the largest. In the corner is a scale which tells how many miles are represented by an inch on the map. If you measure the maps, and use the scale, you can find out how long each island is. You can find out how wide each island is. You can find out how far apart the islands are.

The chief bays and harbors of each island are

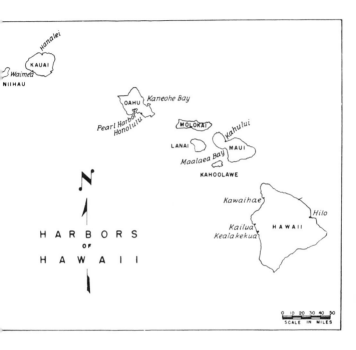

named on the outline map. The map shows you where these bays and harbors are. Some of the islands have no good bays or harbors. Some of them have several good bays or harbors.

CHAPTER THREE

Location of the Hawaiian Islands

THE HAWAIIAN ISLANDS are in the Pacific Ocean. We say they are *located* in the Pacific Ocean.

The Pacific Ocean covers a great part of the surface of the earth. It touches the shores of the four continents: Asia, Australia, North America and South America.

There are many, many islands in the Pacific Ocean. Islands which are located near each other make up an *island group*.

The map on the next page shows part of the Pacific Ocean. It shows the Pacific coasts of four continents. It shows some of the Pacific island groups, particularly the islands in which Polynesian people live.

The Hawaiian Islands are north of the other Polynesian islands. They are far from any continent. They are far from other island groups.

In the corner of this map is a scale. A great many miles are represented by one inch on this map. You can use this scale just as you used the others.

12

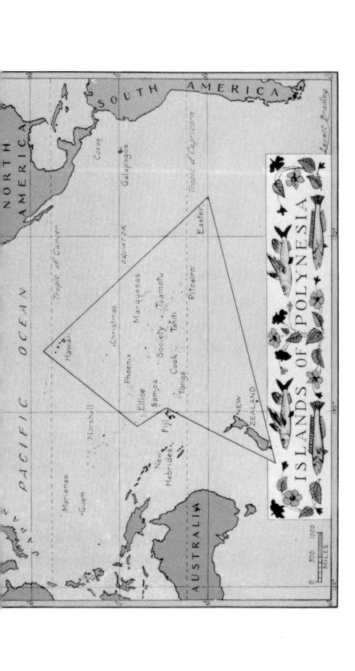

CHAPTER FOUR

The Polynesians Come to Hawaii

LONG, LONG AGO, no one lived in the Hawaiian Islands. They were so far away from any other land that no one knew about them.

People were living in other Polynesian island groups south of Hawaii. These people were brave and skillful seamen. One day, some of them went north over the ocean. They happened to find the Hawaiian Islands. They stayed there to live.

The Polynesians who found Hawaii did not find many food plants growing there. Only certain kinds of plants could have been there.

Plants which grow from seeds carried by the wind, or dropped by birds, might have been there. Plants which had been carried by ocean currents might have been there.

Plants and trees which grow from slips or shoots could not have been there. People had to bring these, carrying them carefully so that they would not die on the long voyage.

Perhaps the first Polynesians found the hala or

pandanus tree growing in Hawaii. Hala fruit can be eaten.

Perhaps the ti plant was there. Its root can be eaten.

TI PLANT

Perhaps certain ferns which can be eaten were there.

The first settlers in Hawaii got along with the few food plants they found growing there. Many years passed. Other Polynesians made the long voyage to Hawaii. Later travelers brought taro, bananas, sugar cane, yams and sweet potatoes to plant. They

COCONUT PALMS AND HALA TREES

brought the ohia ai or mountain apple, the bread-fruit tree and the coconut palm. They also brought small animals—chickens, pigs and dogs.

Some of the new settlers in Hawaii visited their old home in the south. They went south for food plants. They went south to ask other people to return with them to Hawaii.

Paao was a chief who went from Hawaii to ask chiefs to return with him to Hawaii. An old Hawaiian song or chant tells how, when Paao's canoes came near the southern islands, a chanter with him called out to Lonokaeho, the chief of the island, saying:

> "O Lono, O Lono, O Lonokaeho!
> Here are the canoes, get on board!
> Come along and dwell in Hawaii-with-the-green-back!
> A land that was found in the ocean,
> That was thrown up from the sea,
> From the very depths of Kanaloa!
> The canoes touch the shore! Come on board!
> Sail to Hawaii, an island!
> An island is Hawaii,
> An island is Hawaii, for Lonokaeho to dwell on."

Lonokaeho did not go to Hawaii, but other chiefs returned with Paao.

The long voyages were made in little ships. The hull of a Polynesian ship was made of two large canoes hollowed from great trees. A platform was built to join the two canoes. A little house was built on the platform to shelter some of the travelers. Masts for sails were set in place. Paddlers sat in each canoe to paddle the ships along. When the wind was blowing from the right direction, the sails were raised. They helped to carry the ship over the ocean.

Polynesians, traveling in ships like this, made many voyages back and forth over the ocean. Then the long voyages stopped. For five hundred years, no new settlers came to Hawaii, and no Hawaiian visited other lands.

CHAPTER FIVE

Mountains and Volcanoes

THE HAWAIIAN ISLANDS are not low and flat, but are what we call high islands. They have many mountains, standing high above the sea. A *mountain* is like a hill, only it is much higher than a hill. A row of mountains is called a *mountain range*.

Outline maps do not tell you anything about mountains. We use other kinds of maps to show mountains. The kind used here we call *perspective* maps. This one shows how the islands in the group would look, if you could look down at them from a place fifty miles in the air.

On the next page are perspective maps of the different islands of the Hawaiian group. The first map shows Kauai and Niihau. The one mountain you see on the island of Kauai is named Waialeale. The next map on the same page shows Oahu. Oahu has two ranges of mountains. One is the Koolau Range. The other is the Waianae Range.

The third map on page 19 shows Maui, Lanai, Kahoolawe and Molokai.

Maui is made up of two mountain masses, one

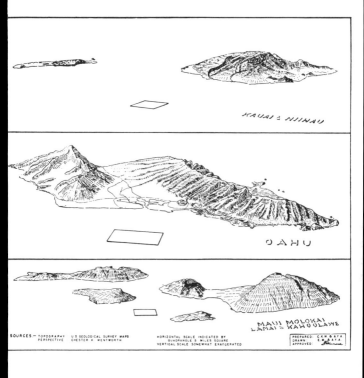

SOURCES— TOPOGRAPHY   U.S GEOLOGICAL SURVEY MAPS   HORIZONTAL SCALE INDICATED BY   PREPARED: C.K.W. & A.T.A.
PERSPECTIVE   CHESTER K. WENTWORTH   QUADRANGLE 5 MILES SQUARE   DRAWN: E.M. & A.T.A.
VERTICAL SCALE SOMEWHAT EXAGGERATED   APPROVED:

much higher than the other. The high mountain is Haleakala.

Haleakala is 10,000 feet high. The lower mountains are the West Maui Mountains.

The maps show you that one end of Molokai is

much higher than the other. They show you that Lanai and Kahoolawe stand like hills in the ocean. These two islands do not have high mountains.

On page 21 is a perspective map of Hawaii. Hawaii has very high mountains. The two highest, each 14,000 feet high, are Mauna Kea and Mauna Loa. They are so high that there is snow on their tops, or *summits,* most of the year. Hualalai, another mountain on Hawaii, is 8,000 feet high. The lowest mountains of Hawaii are the Kohala Mountains.

Mountains are made in different ways, but all the mountains of the Hawaiian Islands were made by volcanoes. The islands were built from the bottom of the sea by volcanoes. Lava flowed out over the floor of the ocean. Slowly the lava was piled up. After a very long time, lava rock showed above the sea. The volcanoes kept on building the islands, until they stood high above the ocean.

There are two active volcanoes on Hawaii. They are still building that island. The black lines on the perspective map of Hawaii show the lava flows which may be seen today. We say that Hawaii is the youngest island because it is still growing.

The Hawaiians did not understand volcanoes. They made a story to explain them. They said that there was a Volcano Goddess named Pele. She lived first, they said, on Kauai, the oldest island. She

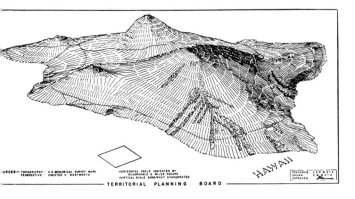

moved from there to find new homes. Finally, they said, she moved to the island of Hawaii, to live forever.

Here is part of an old Hawaiian song. It gives Pele's words when she left the other islands and started for Hawaii:

> "Farewell to thee, Maui, farewell!
> Farewell to thee, Molokai, farewell!
> Farewell to thee, Lanai, farewell!
> Farewell to thee, Kahoolawe, farewell!
> We stand ready to travel.
> Hawaii, it seems, is the land
> On which we shall dwell forever."

Active volcanoes are not always sending lava over the land. The volcanoes of Hawaii are often

21

quiet for months, or years. When the lava rises in the deep pits, and runs over their edges, we say that the volcano is *erupting*. The old Hawaiians said that Pele was angry when the volcano erupted.

Here is part of an old song describing an eruption from Kilauea, one of the active volcanoes of Hawaii:

> "The fire of the woman Pele
> Is burning in the uplands of Puna;
> By the white snow of Mauna Kea,
> The smoke darkens the heavens . . .
> The sound of the round stones is heard . . .
> The axe with the red binding is striking . . .
> Kilauea is consumed by fire,
> Puna is darkened by the bitter rain,
> Stifling is the smoke from the pit,
> The strong offensive smoke of Pele."

The sound of the round stones is the way the Hawaiian poet described thunder.

The axe with the red binding is the way he described lightning.

The bitter rain is the way he described the ashes falling on the land.

The fire of Pele is the way he described the volcano fires.

The islands of Hawaii, with their many high mountains, were really "thrown up from the sea,

THE FIRE **OF** PELE

thrown up from the very depths," as another old poem said. There was no angry Pele, but there were volcanoes which built the islands from the floor of the ocean. These volcanoes built two of the highest island mountains in the world. One of them, Mauna Loa, is still being built.

23

CHAPTER SIX

The Formation of Soil

VOLCANOES SEND OUT melted rock, or *lava*. The path which this moving lava takes is the *lava flow*. The lava quickly cools and hardens into rock. The rocks are slowly broken down into soil.

Rain helps to break down the rocks. In old lava flows, in dry parts of the Islands, there is much less soil than in the newer lava flows in rainy districts. Also, fewer plants grow there.

The pounding waves of the sea help to break down lava rocks along the shore. Streams wear away the rocks and help to break them down. Regular winds and rain together help to break down the hard rocks.

The wind blows seeds into cracks in the rocks. These seeds sprout and grow. The plant roots split the rocks. One of the first plants to grow on Hawaiian lava flows is the fern.

Ferns are protected by woolly scales. The seeds of the ohia lehua tree, blown by the wind, fall into these woolly scales and sprout. The ohia lehua tree

TREE FERNS AND OHIA LEHUA TREES
GROWING IN AN OLD CRATER

begins to grow. It sends its roots into the rocks, and splits them. Leaves fall into the cracks. Some of them stay there. They are dampened by the rain. They rot. They form what we call *leaf mold*. Leaf mold is good food for plants.

The first ohia lehua tree growing on a lava flow is small and twisted. When there is a little more soil,

the tree fern appears. The tree fern has large scales.
Many ohia lehua seeds sprout and grow in these
large scales. Many new trees appear. Their roots
split the rocks. Their leaves fall into the large cracks,
to rot and form more soil.

Other plants, whose seeds are dropped by birds,
or blown by the wind, find root and grow. After
many years, a forest is growing out of the thin soil
which has been formed. The forest trees drop their
leaves, and thicker soil is formed.

In such ways—by wind, rain, streams, waves and
growing plants—the rocks of the Hawaiian Islands
were broken down. The new lava flows of the island
of Hawaii are still being broken down in such ways.

An old Hawaiian poem tells in a few lines what
happened:

"Born was the island—
It budded, it leafed, it grew, it was green,
This island blossomed.
It was Hawaii,
This Hawaii was an island . . .
Hawaii appeared an island."

MAUNA KEA

CHAPTER SEVEN

Mountains and Their Effects

IF YOU CLIMB any Hawaiian mountain, you will find that the air becomes cooler. The higher you go, the colder it is. This is true of all mountains.

As you climb a Hawaiian mountain, you find that the trees and plants are different from those near

27

the shores. Trees and plants which will not grow near the shore where it is always warm will grow on the sides or *slopes* of the mountains.

If you climb high enough, you come to a place where very few trees and plants are found. It is too cold for them. This is true of all mountains. Trees and plants cannot grow on the cold, snow-covered summits of high mountains.

In Hawaii, the wind blows from the northeast nearly every month of the year. These winds are the *trade winds*. The trade winds blow over many miles of sea. They gather moisture from the ocean. The moisture forms into clouds, which are blown along by the wind.

The trade wind clouds are blown against the high mountain slopes of the Islands. They are forced upward. They become cooled. They cannot hold as much moisture when they are cooled as they could when warm. Warm air can hold more moisture than cool air can.

The clouds drop the moisture which they cannot hold. It falls as rain. The rain falls on the northeast side of the Islands. This is the *windward* side; that is, the side toward which the regular winds blow. The windward mountain slopes are the rainiest parts of the Islands.

When the winds reach the opposite side of the

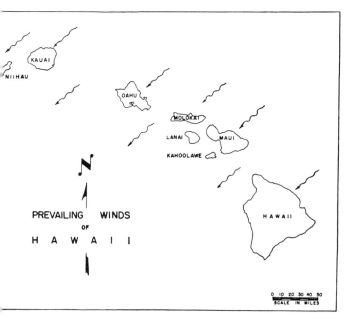

KAUAI

NIIHAU

OAHU

MOLOKAI

LANAI

MAUI

KAHOOLAWE

N

PREVAILING WINDS
OF
H A W A I I

HAWAII

0 10 20 30 40 50
SCALE IN MILES

Islands, the *leeward* side, they are not carrying as
much moisture as they carried before. Little rain
falls on the leeward side of the Hawaiian Islands.

The mountains of Hawaii were important to the
Hawaiian people. Many trees and plants which
they needed grew only on the mountain slopes. The
mountains were high enough to cause the clouds
to drop their moisture. Some of the water soaked

into the ground, watering trees and plants. Some formed into streams of fresh water for the people to use.

Old Hawaiian poems often mention the rain, especially the heavy rain of the rainiest places. Here is one about the rain in Koolau, the Hawaiian name for the windward side:

"Coming is the rain-cloud of Koolau,
  Coming is the rain-cloud of Koolau . . .
  The streams are full when it rains . . .
  The water flows—it overflows,
  The tapering rain that falls upon the stems of the
    ferns!"

Here is a song about two chiefs, wandering in the rainy forests of Kauai:

"Lonely and deserted . . .
  Two continued tramping in the forest . . .
  Loin cloth of ferns was made,
  Ti leaf was broken and worn at the back . . .
  Thus were two sheltered from the rain . . .
  We ate of the ripe pandanus in our wan-
    derings . . .
  Thus did we two wander along . . .
  Through the heavy and wind-blown rain.

One rain was from the highlands,
One rain was from the lowlands,
One rain was from the east,
One rain was from the west . . .
The rain drops danced in the forest,
The rain in the forest fell low,
The rain in the forest danced about,
The rain in the forest fell softly,
The rain in the forest was like mist,
The rain in the forest fell from all sides,
The rain in the forest fell at the back.
The rain cut furrows in the forest . . .
In the uplands."

CHAPTER EIGHT

The Winds

PEOPLE LIVING in Hawaii today speak of two kinds of wind. They speak of the trade wind which always blows from the northeast. They speak of the Kona wind which blows from the south. The trade winds are cool and pleasant. The Kona winds bring unpleasant warm weather. This is all that the people of Hawaii know about the winds today.

Long ago, the Hawaiians paid more attention to the winds than do people living in the Islands today. Little winds which people do not notice today were important to the Hawaiians when they paddled their canoes through the rough waters between the islands. A little change in the wind made a great difference in the fishing.

The old Hawaiians had many names for the little winds of each island. An old song names 19 separate winds which belonged to the island of Hawaii. It names 46 winds which belonged to Kauai and Niihau. It names 46 which belonged to Molokai and Maui. Sixteen of these winds belonged only to Halawa on Molokai.

LISTENING TO A CHANTER

The Hawaiians did not understand winds. They made a story to explain them. There was a chief, they said, whose grandmother ruled the winds. When she died, she left the winds in a calabash. Her grandson was given this calabash. He was taught the names of the winds, and the way to call them. When he lifted the cover, and called the winds in the right way, the winds came out.

The story tells how he, and later, his son, used

the calabash of winds. It helped them to win canoe
races. It helped them against their enemies.

Here is part of the song about the winds of the
islands of Hawaii:

> "There they are! There they are!
> There they are!
> The hard winds of Kohala,
> The short, sharp winds of Kawaihae,
> The fine mist of Waimea . . .
> The soft wind of Kiholo,
> The calm of Kona . . .
> The damp wind of Kapalilua,
> The whirlwind of Kau,
> The dust-driven wind of Naalehu,
> The smoke-driven wind of Kilauea."

The many names of the separate winds help to
show you how well the Hawaiian people knew their
islands. When every little breeze had its own name,
you can imagine that everything else was carefully
named. This was true.

The forests, the valleys, the mountains, the water-
falls, the streams, the bays, the channels, the beaches
--each had its own name. The place names were repeated in the songs and chants of the people. The listeners knew what was meant when a place was men-
tioned in a song. They knew their islands.

HAU TREE

CHAPTER NINE

Using Plants and Trees of Different Regions

MANY DIFFERENT plants and trees grow in the Hawaiian Islands. Some of them grow best along sandy beaches and in the lowlands. Some grow best in dry forests. Some grow best in wet forests. Some grow best on mountain slopes, or along the high

sides of valleys. Some grow best in rocky places, while others need deeper soil.

The Hawaiians knew which plant or tree was best for every use. Their use of different plants and trees from different places is seen in the making of the canoe.

A single canoe was hollowed from a single tree trunk. When a Hawaiian wished to build a canoe, he had to find the right kind of tree. He looked for a tall, straight koa tree.

Koa trees grow both in wet and dry forests. They grow in the uplands and mountains which are from 600 to 5000 feet high. In the dry forests, the tree has low branches, and the trunk is often twisted. This kind of koa would not make a good canoe.

The koa of the wet forests often grows very tall, and has no branches within 40 feet of the ground. This was the kind of tree needed for a canoe. The canoe builder had to go to the wet forests to find the right kind of tree.

A rim was fastened to the canoe to make the sides higher. The rim might be made of the yellow wood of the ahakea tree. This tree was found in the wet forests, below a height of 2000 feet. Sometimes the rim was made of breadfruit wood. The breadfruit tree grows best in the lowlands.

The Hawaiian single canoe always had an out-

BREADFRUIT

rigger. The outrigger was made of three pieces of wood. These were the outrigger float, and the two curving poles which connected the float to the canoe.

The outrigger float was made of the very light wood of the wiliwili tree. This tree grows best in the hottest, driest districts, below a height of 1500 feet.

37

A KOA OF THE DRY FOREST

BLOSSOMS OF THE WILIWILI

The two curving pieces which joined the out-rigger float to the canoe were made of hau wood. Hau grows best along the beaches and in the low-lands of the Hawaiian Islands.

The pieces forming the outrigger were tied to-gether with *sennit*. Sennit is cord made from coco-

KUKUI LEAVES, FLOWERS AND NUTS

nut fiber. The outrigger was tied to the canoe with sennit. The rim was tied to the hull with sennit.

The canoe was polished. Many different materials were used to polish the canoe. Some of them

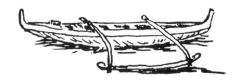

were coconut husk, lava rock and coral rock from the sea.

Below the yellow rim, the canoe was painted black. The black paint was made in different ways. Sometimes bark of the kukui tree, which grows best in narrow, rocky valleys, was well pounded. This made a beautiful black paint. Sometimes certain plants were burned until they blackened. The blackened material was mixed with water, and with pounded ti root. The ti root helped to make the color fast.

Canoe paddles were often made from the koa tree which grew in dry forests. Sails were made of mats plaited from the leaves of the hala tree. This tree grows along sandy beaches and in the lowlands.

Thus, to make one canoe, men gathered materials from the wet forests, the dry forests, the valley sides, the lowlands, the beaches and the driest districts of the Islands.

Besides canoes, the Hawaiians made many other things. Always special plants and trees, growing best in some places and not found in others, were used to made particular articles. The people went from the mountains to the sea to get the different materials which they used.

CHAPTER TEN

From the Mountains to the Sea

LONG, LONG AGO, each island of the Hawaiian group was divided into districts. Nearly all the districts ran from the mountain top to the deep sea.

The people living in a district had the right to take from it the things they needed. If a man wished to build a canoe, he could go anywhere in his district to get the materials he needed. If he wished to build a house, he could go anywhere in his district to get the wood and other materials he needed.

No person could go into another district and take its products. Very wet districts had no wiliwili trees. Men who lived there traded something they had for the wiliwili wood which they needed for outrigger floats. Very dry districts had no koa trees for canoes. Men who lived there traded something they had for the koa wood which they needed to make canoes.

Only a few places had the right kind of lava from which stone tools could be made. The best stone was found high up the slopes of Mauna Kea. The

tool makers of Mauna Kea needed food which was raised in warmer places. They needed fish. They traded their stone tools for the things which they needed.

The island of Lanai had little water. Wet-land taro, the chief vegetable food of the Hawaiians, could not be raised there. But there was very good fishing along the coast of Lanai. Men who lived there traded their fish for the food raised on near-by Maui.

If a man did not like his district, he could move into another one. As long as he lived in a district, he could take the products of his district, and only those products.

If the district had a stream of water, the men raised wet-land taro. They could not take all the water they wanted for their fields. Water was one thing they could not take freely. There were many rules about the use of water. Water was important because it was needed for growing wet-land taro.

LLEY

CHAPTER ELEVEN

Streams, Valleys and Water

THE POLYNESIANS who found the Hawaiian Islands could not have stayed there to live if they had not found fresh water there. Ocean water is salt. People cannot drink salt water. Animals cannot drink it. Most plants cannot use it. People, animals and land plants must have fresh water.

There are many streams of fresh water in the Hawaiian Islands. Most of them are in valleys. A *valley* is low land between hills or mountains.

Valley streams flow from the higher part of the valley to the lower part. The place at which the stream begins is its *source*.

If you start at the source of a Hawaiian valley stream, and follow the stream down, you find that it runs into the sea. The place at which it enters the sea is its *mouth*.

At the mouth of many of the Hawaiian streams are bays and sandy beaches. Valleys with streams, bays and beaches were good places for the people to live. On page 44 is a picture of such a valley.

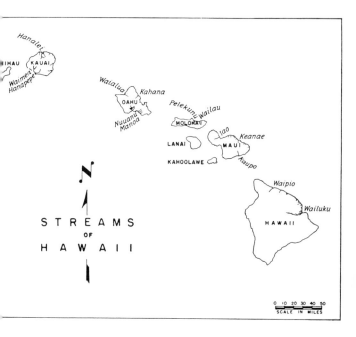

Some of the Hawaiian valley streams are shorter than the one shown in the picture. Some of them are longer. None of them is very long. Very long streams, or *rivers*, are found on continents. Some of the Hawaiian streams are called rivers, but they are not real rivers.

Some Hawaiian valley sides are steeper than

those shown in the picture. Some of the valleys are narrower. Some Hawaiian valleys have rocky shores and no beaches. Most of them have streams.

On page 47 is a map of the Hawaiian Islands. It shows the streams and valleys, and names some of them.

The map tells you where the streams are. It also shows you that many places have no streams. Where did the people who lived there get water?

Sometimes they dug shallow holes in which rain water was collected. Sometimes they found natural pools of rain water a few miles from their homes. Sometimes they found fresh-water springs. A *spring* is water rising from below the ground. Some springs were in the valleys. Others were near the shore.

Water was so important to the Hawaiian people that they had many songs about the magic water of Kane, the water of life. Here is part of one of these old songs:

THE WATER OF KANE

One question I put to you;
Where is the water of Kane?
Yonder on the mountain peak,
On the ridges steep,
In the valleys deep,

Where the rivers sweep:
There is the water of Kane.

This question I ask of you;
Where is the water of Kane?
Yonder, at sea, on the ocean,
In the driving rain,
In the heavenly bow,
In the mist, in the rain—
There is the water of Kane.

One question I put to you;
Where, where is the water of Kane?
Up on high is the water of Kane,
In the heavenly blue,
In the cloud,
In the sacred cloud of the gods;
There is the water of Kane.

One question I ask of you;
Where flows the water of Kane?
Deep in the ground, in the gushing spring,
In the spring, a well-spring of water,
A water of magic power—
The water of Life!
Life! O, give us this life!

CHAPTER TWELVE

Wet-Land Taro

THE HAWAIIANS raised their chief vegetable food, wet-land taro, wherever there was plenty of fresh water. Wet-land taro can be grown in the lowlands, in places through which fresh water is always moving.

Taro was raised in small fields called patches. Men built strong walls around each patch. These walls were made to hold the water in the patch.

Water for the taro patches usually came from streams, though spring water was also used. Men built dams in the stream. A *dam* is a wall across a stream. It holds the water back. The water collects in a pool above the dam.

Men built ditches to bring water from the pools to the taro patches. The Hawaiian name for such a ditch is *auwai*. An auwai might be very long, or it might be short.

Taro patches were close together. Only the walls separated them. Water was allowed to run first into one patch, then into another.

Every person who raised wet-land taro had to have water. No one might take too much. The district chief told each man just how long he could let water run into his patch. The district chief gave

USING THE O–O

the most water to the men who worked the longest on the dams and auwais.

Before men planted taro, they dug the ground in the patch with a pointed stick of hard wood. The digging stick was sometimes made of alahee wood.

Often it was made of kauila wood. Both of these hardwood trees were found in the dry forests.

RIPE TARO WHICH HAS BEEN GATHERED

The digging stick was called an o-o. It was the only field tool the Hawaiians had.

Just before the taro was planted, the soil of the patch was softened by treading. That is, men tramped it with their feet. The patch was filled with

water the night before the treading. The day for treading the patch was a holiday.

Men, women and children helped to tread the patch. The owner provided a feast. Everyone wore leis, and everyone helped. All the people waded in, tramping here and there, and stirring the mud with their feet.

Next day the patch was planted. The planter had his taro slips ready. They were carefully chosen slips, from the best taro.

The slips were planted in the soft soil of the taro patch. After this was done, bananas, sugar cane and ti plants were set out along the banks.

When the first taro leaves appeared, the farmer gathered them. He lighted a fire. He cooked the leaves. He offered them to Kane with a prayer. Here is part of his prayer:

> "O Kane-of-the-living-waters!
> Here are the first fruits of our taro.
> Return, O god, and grant us food!
> Food for my family,
> Food for the pigs,
> Food for the dogs.
> Grant success to me . . .
> In farming, in fishing, in housebuilding—
> Until I am bent with age."

As the taro grew, it was so carefully weeded that not a single weed was left. After the weeding, the farmer prayed to Ku. Here is part of his prayer:

"O Ku . . . may our taro leaves bear in abundance!
O Ku . . . may our taro have stalks like the banana!
O Ku . . . may our taro have stems like the a-pe!
O Ku . . . may our taro have leaves like the banana!
O Ku . . . let them cover a man hidden in our taro!"

A feast was made when the first ripe taro was cooked and eaten. Some of the food was offered to the gods with prayers. Here is part of one prayer:

"O god, O Ku . . . O Ku-of-the-long-cloud,
O Ku-of-the-short-cloud, O Ku-of-the-hanging-cloud,
O Ku-of-the-very-dark-cloud-of-the-heavens . . .
Here is food, here is fish, here is food . . .
Grant life, grant life to the ruling chief,
Grant life to the lesser chiefs,
Grant life to the people,
Grant life to me, the mighty farmer,
Grant life to my family,
Grant life to my household,
Grant life to my food plants,
Dig deep that the earth may live . . .
Eat, eat."

CHAPTER THIRTEEN

Making Poi

THE HAWAIIANS made taro into poi. The first step in making poi was to cook the taro. Nearly all Hawaiian cooking was done in an underground oven. The Hawaiian name for this oven is *imu.*

The imu was used because the Hawaiians could do very little cooking over an open fire. They had no fireproof cooking pots. They could broil fish on sticks over an open fire, but they could not cook most of their food this way.

To make an imu, men dug a hole in the ground. They lined it with stones. Every stone used in an imu had to be one which would not burst when it was very hot.

A fire was built in the imu. The Hawaiians lighted a fire by rubbing a stick of hard wood quickly back and forth in a groove made in a larger, softer piece of wood. When the sparks came, they were caught on bits of dried grass or bark cloth.

More stones were put into the fire in the imu. The fire was kept burning until all the stones were very hot.

MAKING FIRE

When the wood in the imu had burned, men put thick layers of damp banana and ti leaves on the hot stones. The damp leaves began to steam. They did not burn because they were damp.

The food to be cooked was put on the leaves. It was covered with layers of damp banana and ti leaves. The imu was finally covered with earth to keep the steam in. The food was left to steam until it was cooked.

Many things were cooked at the same time. The imu was opened so that the food which cooked

fastest might be taken out. It was closed again to let the rest of the food cook.

After about three hours, the taro was taken out. Men peeled the taro with clean opihi shells.

The poi maker brought out his poi board, his poi pounder and a bowl of fresh water. The poi board was long and heavy. It was hollowed a little in the center.

Poi pounders were made of stone. Some were heavier than others. They were not always the same shape. A gourd water bowl, or a wooden water bowl, was used.

The poi maker sat at one end of the poi board. He took some of the cooked, peeled taro and put it on the board. He wet the face of the poi pounder. He lifted the pounder and brought it down on the cooked taro. He did this over and over, always wetting the face of the pounder between strokes.

By and by the taro on the board was pounded into a thick, heavy paste. This was called *paiai*. Paiai which was going to be kept for several days was wrapped in ti leaves. It was put in covered gourd containers. The covers kept the paiai from hardening. The gourds were slung in nets so that they could be hung up.

Part of the paiai was mixed with water until it

became a thinner paste. This thin paste was 'poi.
Poi was put into bowls. It was ready to eat.

Fresh poi is sweet. It soon begins to sour. If it is
kept too long, it is too sour to eat. Paiai does not
sour for a long time. Every few days, fresh poi was
mixed from the paiai kept in the gourds.

Cooking was not done every day. The imu was
lighted when the family had eaten the food which
had been cooked a few days before.

Hawaiian men did the hard work of raising taro.
They did the hard work of preparing the imu. They
usually pounded the taro. Women sometimes helped
with the pounding. If they did, they used the
smaller, lighter poi pounders.

When the first taro ripened in his taro patch, the
farmer said a prayer. Part of this prayer tells you
in a few lines about the preparation of poi:

"O Ku, our taro is ripe.
  In the morning our taro shall be pulled up,
  Fastened into a bundle, taken home.
  The oven for our taro shall be lighted.
  The taro shall be cooked in the oven,
  The oven opened, the taro peeled.
  The taro shall be pounded and placed in a cala-
      bash.
  The food shall be softened, O Ku. . . ."

POUNDING TARO

JULIETTE MAY FRASER

CHAPTER FOURTEEN

Products of the Dry Lands

THE MAP in Chapter 11 shows you that there were many places in the Hawaiian Islands which had no streams. Such places sometimes had springs from which the people could get enough water for wet-land taro. But if there were no streams and no springs, wet-land taro could not be raised.

People who lived in dry districts planted dry-land taro, sweet potatoes, yams, bananas and sugar cane. They hoped that enough rain would fall so that their food plants would grow well. Sugar cane and bananas needed the most rain.

The dry-land farmer prayed when he made his o-o. Since the o-o was often made of kauila wood, he said:

> "A kauila stick to be used on the plains,
> To plant sweet potatoes for food,
> Dry-land taro for food,
> Bananas for food . . .
> And sugar cane for food."

On the day sweet potatoes were to be planted, in a

HAWAIIAN BANANAS

district where the soil was soft, the men wore leis. All the men dressed alike. All the women dressed alike. Each man carried his o-o. All the men and women went to the fields.

A line was stretched to mark the first straight row. The men dug holes for the slips on each side of the cord. They made the holes far enough apart so that the plants would have plenty of room.

Women followed along the row. They carried the slips, and put them in the holes. The soil was made into a little hill around each plant.

The plants were left alone until they had taken root. Then the hills were stirred with an o-o to soften the earth. When the vines grew and spread over the ground, the earth was softened again.

When bananas were planted, the farmer dug large, deep holes. He brought the young banana plants. He put them into the deep holes, praying all the time. He prayed that each banana plant would grow very large, saying:

> "The great banana!
> The great banana!
> It will yield ten hands,
> The bunch cannot be carried . . .
> It will take two men to carry it
> With difficulty."

If enough rain did not fall, the dry-land farmer prayed to Ku to send rain. Here is part of the prayer:

"O Ku-of-the-long-cloud
  Ku-of-the-short-cloud,
  Ku-of-the-very-dark-cloud-of-the-heavens . . .
  Drop down a heavy shower,
  A very heavy rain . . .
  Let the rains bring relief to my field,
  By drenching it from that end to this,
  From that side to this,
  Thoroughly wetting it,
  So that our garden will be fruitful.
  Let our plants grow well,
  So that you may eat of the food with me and my
      family,
  So that you may partake of the bananas with me
      and my family,
  So that you may wear bark cloth with me and my
      family."

CHAPTER FIFTEEN

The Seas

THE TWO CHIEF foods of the Hawaiians were poi
and fish. Before we can tell about ways of fishing,
we must tell something about the seas near the Hawaiian Islands, and the ocean itself.

The ocean is not a smooth, still body of water. It
has waves. It has tides. It has currents. All these
make a difference in fishing.

People who live near the ocean know that the
depth of the water changes during the day. Twice
in each twenty-four hours, the water near the shore
rises. Twice in each twenty-four hours, the water
falls. When it rises, the tide is coming in. When it
falls, the tide is going out. The water near the shore
is deepest at high tide. It is shallowest at low tide.

Tides are regular movements of ocean water toward the shore, and away from the shore. When the
tide is coming in, there is a current or movement of
water toward the land. When the tide is going out,
the current goes toward the sea.

At certain times each month, and at certain sea-

A ROCKY HEADLAND

sons of the year, the high tides are higher than they are at other times. The low tides are lower.

Winds blowing over the ocean make the water rise in waves. The stronger the wind, the higher the waves. The waves roll along. When they strike land, they break. Sometimes they spread out gently on a sandy beach. Sometimes they break heavily on

a steep beach. Sometimes they strike a cliff and break in a cloud of white spray.

Waves are not all the same, but we do not have words to describe different waves. We speak of high waves, or small waves. That is about all we say about waves.

The Hawaiians studied waves, and they used many words to describe them. They had special names for every part of a wave, for every kind of wave. Just as they named the many different winds, so they named the waves.

The Hawaiians had a special name for the wave which breaks before it reaches the shore. They had a special name for the wave which spreads out gently on a sandy beach. They had a special name for the back of a wave, and another for the foam of a wave. They had names for waves which rose high before breaking, and for those which curled over and broke. The wave which dashed against a cliff had its own name.

Winds blowing over the ocean often make the surface waters move in the direction of the wind. This movement of ocean water is a *current*. The moving surface water makes the deeper water move more slowly in the same direction.

When the wind changes, the current does not change as quickly as you might expect. This is be-

cause the deep water current is strong enough to keep the surface water moving for some time against the wind. The surface of the sea grows rough when this happens.

Water between islands which are close together is called a *channel*. The channel waters of the Hawaiian Islands are often very rough. It is hard to manage small boats or canoes in these rough channel waters.

Tides, waves and currents are very important to island people. They make a difference to fishermen. They make a difference to men traveling in canoes. Island people must know a great deal about the waters around their islands.

The Hawaiians knew all the seas near their shores. They often described them in their songs. Here is part of an old song about the seas of Oahu:

"The sea for surf-riding is at Kahaloa . . .
 The sea for casting the net is at Kalia . . .
 The sea of many harbors is at Puuloa . . .
 A sea that blows up small bait-fish
 Is the sea of Ewa so calm
 The great Ewa lands of Laakona . . .
 The sea of Heeia is mottled . . .
 The sea that calls is at Kualoa,
 The sea that wears away is at Kaaawa,
 The wild sea is at Kahana."

Here are some more descriptions of different seas near the Islands:

"Waialua, land of the sounding sea . . .
A voice that reaches Wahiawa . . .
Our ears are stunned by this voice—
The voice of old Ocean!"

"Kaena Point flies on its way
Like a sea bird in fair weather . . .
Like the lash of the sea bird's wings
Is the curl of the breaking wave
In the channel of Ieie."

"The voice of Puna's sea resounds
Through the echoing hala groves;
And lehua trees cast their bloom."

"Makapuu climbs to the sky . . .
While Ocean pounds and breaks at its base—
The sea, the home of the gods."

CHAPTER SIXTEEN

The Reefs

NEAR THE SHORES of some of the islands of the Hawaiian group are lines of rocks. They are close to the surface of the sea. These lines of rocks are *reefs*.

Most of the reefs of the Hawaiian Islands are made of coral rock. Certain little sea animals can live in warm, shallow water. They cannot move about. They die where they have lived. Their tiny bones harden. They are pressed together by the weight of the water above them. In this way, what we call *coral* is formed.

New animals grow, live and die. The coral reef is built up in this way.

There are no coral reefs near the island of Hawaii. The water around that island is too deep.

In several places, the coral reef ends, and, a little farther along the coast, begins again. This is because the reef is near the mouth of some fresh-water stream. The water which reaches the reef is still fresh. Fresh water kills coral animals.

The most famous and useful break in a reef is the

one caused by the Nuuanu Stream of Oahu. This stream empties into Honolulu harbor. Its fresh waters reach the reef outside the harbor. The break caused by the fresh stream waters is the natural gateway to the best harbor of the Hawaiian group.

Coral rock is not solid. Sometimes it is built up with branches like the branches of a tree. It grows in many different shapes.

Coral reefs have many rocky holes under the water. Squid and eels like to live in such places. Certain fish stay in and around such places.

The coral reefs of the Hawaiian Islands have many important effects. They shut off the shallow water near the shore from the deep sea. Sharks, which do not like shallow water, seldom go inside a reef. Swimmers inside a reef are safe from sharks.

Wherever there is a reef, the waves from the deep sea break at the reef, not on the shore. They roll in gently to the shore. Inside a reef, there is no strong current running back toward the sea. Swimming is safe there for that reason.

The best surf-riding is found where there is a reef. The surf-rider goes to the reef and waits for a wave. He catches the wave just before it breaks. He rides in ahead of it to the shore.

Large ships cannot go over a reef, but a canoe can. A good paddler takes his canoe over a reef in

ALONG A CORAL REEF

much the same way that the surf-rider takes his board to shore.

Many kinds of fish are found only along reefs. People who wade along the reef easily find out how to catch these fish. Expensive nets or lines are not used in reef fishing.

The Hawaiians did a great deal of fishing along the reefs. They enjoyed the sport of surf-riding, which was made possible by the reefs. They were able to take their canoes over a reef. Men, women and children fished and swam safely in the shallow waters protected by reefs.

CHAPTER SEVENTEEN

Fishermen

IN ORDER to get enough food from the sea, the Hawaiians learned to be very good fishermen. A fisherman has to know the seas, the waves, the currents, the tides. He also has to know the habits of different fish.

You know that there are large fish and small fish. You probably know that all kinds of fish do not look alike. But, because fish live in the water where you cannot easily watch them, you may not know that different fish have very different habits.

Some fish live only in shallow water and never go into the deep sea. Others live only in deep water. Some live near sandy shores. Others live near rocky shores and never go far from rocky holes. Some fish are easily caught, while others fight and try hard to get away. Some fish always swim near the surface, while others always swim much deeper. Some fish are found near the shore only at high tide. Others are found only at low tide. Some fish come close when a certain kind of noise is made. Others swim away from the sound of voices or splashing water.

If you want to get mountain apples, you do not walk all over the forest. You go where the mountain apples are. In the same way, the Hawaiians did not go all over the sea, hoping to catch fish. They went where the fish were.

It is easier to find mountain apples than to find fish. How did the Hawaiians do this? They learned the habits of different kinds of fish. They studied the habits of the fish. When they went fishing, they went to the right place. Fish do not live just anywhere in the sea. They have their favorite places, near the shore or in the deep water.

A place where many fish like to go is called a *fishing ground*. A good fisherman knows where the fishing grounds are.

Hawaiian fishermen knew where to go for different kinds of fish. They also knew when to go. They knew whether to go at high tide, or at low tide. They knew whether to go on a calm, sunny day, or in cloudy weather. They knew whether to go early in the morning, or in the evening, or at night.

The fishermen knew just what to use to catch a certain kind of fish. They knew when to take along a fine net, when a coarse one. They knew when to take a small net, when a large one. They knew when to take a very long, strong line, and when to take a shorter one. They knew when to take live bait,

cooked bait or an unbaited, shining hook. They knew when to ask many helpers to go with them, and when to ask a few.

The Hawaiians had a hundred different ways of fishing. They had so many different ways because they knew the different kinds of fish.

Here are some of the things the Hawaiians said about fish:

"The fish have ears. When they hear you say you are going fishing, they run away. So don't say you are going fishing. Don't talk on your way to the fishing grounds. Don't talk after you get there.

"Fish are timid and do not like to be noticed. If you speak out and notice them, they will run away. Don't say, 'There he is!' when the fish enters the net.

"Fish like a clean house. The net, when it is cast into the sea, is a house for the fish. So never step on a net when it is spread out on the ground. Never step on it when it is lying in a bundle."

CHAPTER EIGHTEEN

Inshore Fishing

MEN DID MOST of the fishing. They did all the canoe and reef fishing. Women did some fishing near the shore.

A great many kinds of fish were caught in different ways near the shore, along the rocks and reefs, and in shallow waters. Fishing in such places is called *inshore* fishing.

Canoes were seldom used in inshore fishing, but the fisherman often had to be a good swimmer and diver. Baskets, nets, spears and the bare hands were used in inshore fishing.

One kind of basket was made of fresh vines. It was about a foot deep. On calm, sunny days, at low tide, women waded out to place these baskets, which contained pounded bait. Certain fish liked the smell of the fresh vines, and went into the baskets for the pounded bait which had been placed there. When a number of fish had gone in, the women waded back. They picked up the baskets. They took the fish out and put them into large gourds or baskets. They set the baskets down again in near-by places.

Another kind of basket was used to catch another kind of fish. Before the fisherman tried to take these fish, he fed them for a week or so at a particular

INSHORE FISHING WITH BASKETS

place. He put pieces of cooked taro, sweet potato and breadfruit in a large basket, and set it in the sea. The fish swam in and out of the basket, and ate the food. They soon got used to the basket with its food, and were not afraid of it.

After a few days, the fisherman put the food in another basket. It looked like the first one, but it

was made so that the fish could not get out, once they had entered. The fish swam into the basket to eat. When the basket was full, the fisherman lifted his basket of fine, fat fish from the water.

Small nets fastened to hoops were often used in inshore fishing. These nets were *dip nets*, or *scoop nets*.

Sometimes the fisherman walked along the shore, dipping his scoop net for the fish, or driving them into it with a leafy branch. Sometimes he walked along rocky shores or reefs, using a stick to drive the fish from their rocky hiding-places into the net. Sometimes he used a scoop net when he went torch fishing.

The torch the Hawaiians used was made of dried or cooked kukui nuts. The nuts were wrapped in leaves and fastened to a stick.

On calm, dark nights, men walked out along the reefs. They carried their lighted torches. They walked carefully, so as not to scare the fish. The fish came out when they saw the light. Men sometimes scooped them up in their little nets. Sometimes they speared the fish.

Spears were often used in inshore fishing. Squid were sometimes speared from above, through holes in the rocks. Spears were sometimes used by divers. The diver took a long spear and dived to the bottom

along a rocky shore or reef. With one hand, he held on to a rock at the bottom. In the other, he held his spear. He often speared large fish. Only a very good swimmer and diver, able to stay under water for some time, could fish in this way.

The Hawaiians used several different kinds of lines in inshore fishing. Sometimes the line was short, with a noose in the end. The noose was let down through a hole in the rocks and slipped over

the head of an eel. Sometimes the line had a hook
and bait, and was cast from high, rocky shores.

Small eels were sometimes caught with the bare
hands. A man lay down along the rocks. He held
bait flat on his hand. His fingers were spread apart.
The little eels came out. The man pulled the bait
back toward his wrist. As soon as an eel tried to
reach the bait by putting its head between the man's
fingers, the man removed the bait and brought his
fingers quickly together. The eel was caught. It was
put into a basket.

Certain other fish were caught by hand along
rocky shores, on moonlight nights when the tide was
going out.

Large nets were used for a particular kind of inshore fishing. On sunny days, in calm water, when
the tide was coming in, but not when it was high,
divers placed the large net. They set it so that it
made a bag under the surface.

Smaller nets were placed at the side of the large
net. Long ropes were hung with ti leaves. The ropes
were fastened to the side nets, and stretched out, far
apart, for some distance.

Men in canoes held the ends of the long ropes.
The ti leaves made shadows in the sunny water. Fish
swimming below the surface of the water saw the
shadows. They tried to get away from them. They

would not cross the shadows. They swam in from the shadows toward the one dark and quiet place. That was the large, roomy bag of the net.

When many fish had entered the net, the mouth of the net was drawn together. The net was pulled to shore, and the fish divided. Hundreds of fish were often caught at one time.

This way of fishing is known today as the hukilau. The name comes from the Hawaiian words for *pull* (huki) and *leaf* (lau). The hukilau is done a little differently today, but the idea is the same as the one used by the Hawaiians long ago.

The Hawaiians built fishponds near the shore. The walls were made of stone, carefully laid. They were so well made that many of them may still be seen.

Fish raised in the fishponds belonged to a chief. Ama-ama, or mullet, was one of the kinds of fish kept in the chief's fishponds.

There were strict rules about all inshore fishing. Inshore fishing belonged to the people whose district touched a particular shore. Inshore fishing rights went as far as the reef, or, where there was no reef, to deep water not far from the shore.

At certain times of the year, no fishing might be done at particular places along the shore. This rule was made to protect the fishing.

KLAU

CHAPTER NINETEEN

Deep-Sea Net Fishing

INSHORE FISHING was easy. It was easy for a man to fish with his hands. It was easy to cast a line from a level shore, or from a high, rocky shore. It was easy to use the scoop net. It was easy to take fish in baskets.

A man could easily get enough fish for his family and his guests to eat with their poi, if he did only these simple things. The Hawaiians did not call these things fishing. Real fishing was deep-sea fishing, not inshore fishing.

Deep-sea fishing was exciting. The Hawaiians liked the fun and excitement of fishing in the deep sea. A true island people, they liked the sea.

All the real fishermen, the expert fishermen, were deep-sea fishermen. They used nets of different kinds. They used poles and lines. Sometimes many canoes and many helpers went fishing with the expert. Sometimes the expert went alone, with a few helpers in one canoe.

For one kind of deep-sea net fishing, the expert

looked for a place with a sandy bottom, where many fish gathered. After he had found it, he waited for calm weather.

When the weather was right, the fisherman asked his friends who were fishermen to go with him the next day. He told them he wished divers to go, too. Everyone knew from this just what to do.

The fisherman's friends prepared the large net. They tied stones to its lower edge. They piled the large net, and some smaller ones, in one canoe.

The start was made early in the morning. The head fisherman led the way. He and two other men went first in a long, narrow canoe.

Paddlers paddled the net canoe. Two other canoes, carrying five or six men each, went along. These men were the ones who would let down the nets. Many other canoes went, carrying divers and helpers.

The head fisherman led the way to the fishing ground. He was chewing kukui nut. From time to time, he leaned out and spat the oil from the kukui nuts over the water. The oil covered the ripples made by the paddles. It made the water smooth and clear. The fisherman could look down and see the bottom through the smooth, clear water.

The head fisherman let a stick down into the fishing ground. This stick had been rubbed with coco-

nut oil, kukui nut oil and other strong-smelling things. The smell drew the fish. They gathered near the stick.

When the head fisherman saw the fish gathering, he called to the men to let down the nets. The men let down the big net, weighted with stones. They let down the side nets.

The head fisherman told the divers to go to the bottom. He told them to keep in line, and walk toward the mouth of the net at the right time. One thing the divers did was to drive the fish into the net.

The divers went to the bottom and waited, some distance from the net. The head fisherman drew his stick close to the mouth of the net. The fish followed the stick. They began to enter the net.

The divers walked closer to the net. The head fisherman kept watching. He began to pull the cord of the net when he thought the net was full. The divers helped to lift the lower edge of the net. They threw it over the upper edge.

The men in the canoes pulled in the nets. They emptied them into the canoes. If all the nets were full, many canoes were filled with fish.

Some of the best fish were picked out at once, and sent to shore for the fisherman's wife and children. The rest were brought in more slowly.

When all the canoes reached the shore, the fish

DEEP-SEA FISHERMEN

were divided. Some were given to the divers. The fish in the side nets, even if they were very choice fish, were always given to the divers. Some fish were given to the men who had helped get the nets ready. Some were given to the men who had let down the nets. Some were given to the paddlers. The largest share went to the head fisherman.

If the fisherman fished for a chief, the chief provided everything needed for the fishing trip. The chief then received the largest share of the fish. A fisherman without a master was himself the head. He received more fish than he could possibly use. He traded part of his share for things he needed. He needed many nets and lines. He needed canoes. He traded fish for these things.

When the head fisherman reached the shore, he took two fish in each hand. He offered them to his fish gods. Every deep-sea fisherman had his own fish gods. He believed that his fish gods helped bring the fish to his nets and lines.

The Hawaiians had many other ways of net-fishing in the deep sea. The weighted net placed on the ocean floor was used only to catch fish which swam far below the surface. A different kind of net, and a different method of fishing, were used to catch deep-sea fish which swam near the surface. Flying-fish, for example, were caught with nets thrown out over

the surface, and gathered in by many canoes. No
divers went out when men were going for flying-
fish.

An old Hawaiian story tells something about the
way the deep-sea fisherman made his preparations,
and how he planned the time to start. One day, this
story tells, the chief Kawelo was visiting the chief
Ma-ku-a-ke-ke at Waianae on Oahu. Ma-ku-a-
ke-ke told him about a magic fish which lived in the
Ieie Channel off Kaena Point. They planned to go for
this magic fish at sunrise. Kawelo could not sleep.
He called his friend at midnight:

"O Ma-ku-a-ke-ke!   Hear!   Hear!
  Arise in the night!
  Bestir yourself!   Leave the pebbles!
  Fetch the bait containers,
  The collection of fishhooks,
  The flexible nets,
  And bind them to the top of the outrigger poles,
  Then paddle for the deep sea!
  . . . O great spirit of the current!
    Bear us to Kaena, out to Ieie
  Where we will catch the fish!
  O Ma-ku-a-ke-ke-i-ki-o. . . . !
  Arise in the night!"

Ma-ku-a-ke-ke got up when his friend called him. He looked at the stars. The star which would show it was time to start had not risen, so he went back to sleep. Kawelo called him again. Again Ma-ku-a-ke-ke looked at the stars, and decided it was too early to start. The third time, he saw the star for which he had been waiting, and started.

Here is another poem about the fisherman's preparations:

> "They awoke at midnight . . .
> They hastened and lit the lamps,
> Partook of the food, partook of the food.
> They considered the prospects,
> Measured off the line of the fisherman,
> Fastened on the fishhook securely,
> For the fish, the fish.
> The canoe,
> The paddle,
> The bailer,
> The seating,
> Carrying
> And departing."

CHAPTER TWENTY

Deep-Sea Line Fishing

THE HAWAIIANS caught many kinds of deep-sea fish with lines. Aku was one fish caught with a pole and line. Aku fishing was a great sport.

A large number of the same kind of fish swimming in the same direction in the sea is called a run of fish. Men learned when there was a run of aku by watching the sea birds. These birds eat the small fish which the aku follows. When there were many sea birds flying low and taking fish, the Hawaiians knew that there was a run of aku.

When the fishermen saw the run of aku, they prepared for the day's sport. They wore leis of hala fruit, ilima and lehua. They put on special malos of red or pale yellow.

If live bait was to be used, many helpers were needed, and many canoes went together. Each carried several fishermen with their poles and lines. Some fishermen went in single canoes. Some went in double canoes, with the live bait container fastened between the two canoes.

The head fisherman led the way. He watched the place where the birds flew low. When the canoes came near the place, he called to the paddlers to stop. The paddlers changed their stroke. No matter how many canoes there were, every canoe stopped at the same moment.

"Throw out the bait," the head fisherman called. Helpers threw out the live bait fish, one at a time. The aku leaped for the little fish. They made a splashing sound.

More fish were thrown. The noise of the leaping aku grew louder. When the noise was very loud, the paddlers dipped their paddles. They began to move the canoes.

All the canoes moved in the same direction. Bait fish were thrown all the time. The aku followed the bait fish. Then the fishing poles were held out. When all the poles were held out in a line, the head fisherman called for more bait to be thrown. It was thrown out by the gourdful.

Each fisherman baited his hook. He trailed the baited hook over the surface of the sea. He braced his pole between his legs. He held his pole in one hand, and threw out bait fish with the other. The aku followed, and soon one took the baited hook, instead of the swimming bait.

As soon as a fish was caught, the fisherman drew

AKU FISHING

in his line, rebaited his hook and cast it back. The canoes followed the run of fish until their load of bait fish was gone.

When the canoes came to shore with their load of aku, there was much trading. The fishermen traded their aku for poi, paiai, sweet potatoes, bananas, sugar cane, breadfruit, kapa and mats. Each helper received his share of the catch.

Each fisherman made his prayers and offerings to his fish gods. He bathed, and put on a dry malo and a kapa shawl. He lighted his imu to cook his fish. He enjoyed the feasting which followed the day of fishing.

All his family went to work to clean and salt the remaining fish. Before dawn, some of the men were off to get more bait fish, for another day of aku fishing.

Sometimes the aku fisherman did not use live bait. He used a shining pearl shell hook instead. He drew this over the surface of the water. It looked like a live fish. The aku rose for the fish, and was caught. When this was done, the canoes did not go out together. They went together only when many helpers were needed to throw out the bait fish.

The deep-sea fisherman using a line did not always use a pole. Sometimes he lowered a long, strong line with a strong hook into a fishing ground.

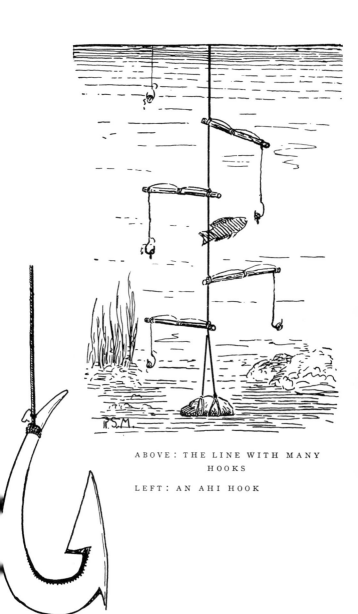

ABOVE: THE LINE WITH MANY
HOOKS

LEFT: AN AHI HOOK

He threw mashed bait into the fishing ground. This spread through the water. It drew the ahi for which he was fishing.

Many ahi swam about, eating the bait spreading through the water. Sooner or later, one took the heavily-baited hook. It tried hard to get away. It swam far and fast. That was why the ahi line was a strong one, often a thousand feet long.

Sometimes the fisherman lowered a line with many hooks, as shown in the picture on page 97. He was not fishing for ahi, but for many smaller fish. He expected to catch a fish on every hook. Such a line might have forty hooks. The fisherman pulled it in when the hooks were full.

The expert fisherman often found secret fishing grounds. If he was going to his secret fishing ground, he started early. He went in a single canoe, with only a few helpers. After he had caught fish in his secret place, he did not pull in his line. He drew it part way up and fastened it to the side of the canoe. Then he paddled far away. When he pulled in his line, no one could tell where he had caught the fish.

The location of a secret fishing ground was a family secret. The expert fisherman told his sons this secret, when they became expert fishermen. He told some other young fisherman if his sons did not become fishermen.

Not everyone could be an expert fisherman. A young man must show that he was worthy to be an expert. He must show his skill. He must learn many things. He must show that he had powerful fish gods who would help him. It was better, the Hawaiians thought, for the sons of fishermen to become experts. Then their father's fish gods would help them.

Many men helped in deep-sea fishing. The helpers were not fishermen. Only the experts, who had been admitted into the company of experts, were fishermen.

CHAPTER TWENTY-ONE

Fish Nets and Lines

Hawaiian fish nets and lines were made of olona fiber. Olona was a plant found in damp places, in rainy districts or in wet mountains. Most of the plants grew on the windward sides of the Islands.

Men who lived in wet districts looked for a good place to plant olona. They cut out the ferns. They

PREPARING OLONA

MAKING A FISHNET

chopped down the trees. They cleared out the
weeds. They planted the shoots of the olona plant.
From time to time, the olona planter weeded the
patch. He pulled up creeping vines which might
choke out the young plants. He kept out the weeds
until the plants were tall and strong enough to keep
out the weeds themselves. In a year or so, the plant
was large enough to use.

Men stripped the bark from the long, straight stems. They rolled the strips carefully and carried them to the lowlands. They soaked the strips in fresh water to loosen the outer bark from the inner bark.

The strips were taken from the water. Several were tied to the end of a long, narrow board. The inner bark, from which the fiber was made, was scraped away with a shell scraper. It was laid in the sun to dry and bleach.

Women took the dry, whitened strips of inner bark which were ready to use. They rolled and twisted them into cord of all sizes. They made very fine cord for fine nets, or for fastening fishhooks to fishlines. They made coarser cord for coarser nets, and for thin fishlines. They made heavy cord for large nets and strong fishlines.

The expert fisherman never made his own fishlines or fishnets. The women of his family made his fishlines. Net makers made his nets. It might take a year or more to make a large, fine net.

Net makers traded pigs or taro or other food for the olona which they needed. Fishermen traded fish for olona and nets.

Olona fiber is very strong. Tests have shown that it is stronger than any other fiber used for rope. Olona nets and lines lasted many years. Salt water

did not hurt them, and the fisherman took good care of his nets and lines.

Lines were rolled, and hung away in a calabash. Nets were treated with the greatest care. When a man had a new net, he offered prayers to his fish gods before using it. When he used an old net for a new purpose, he first offered prayers to his fish gods. When he traded fish for an old net, and used it for the first time, he offered prayers to his fish gods.

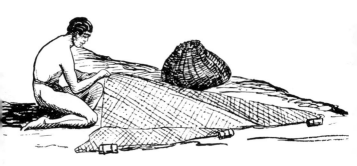

BEGINNING A CA[

THE FOREST

CHAPTER TWENTY-TWO

Beginning a Canoe in the Forest

CANOES WERE very important to the Hawaiians. They were more important than houses, because the Hawaiians spent most of their time out of doors. They were more important than clothing, because the Hawaiians did not need warm clothing. Canoes were more important than other things because the Hawaiians were an island people who loved the sea. Canoes were important because they were used in all the deep-sea fishing which gave the people a great deal of their food.

Canoes were always built by men trained in the work. No one else was allowed to work on a canoe. The work began when the experts went to the wet forests to choose and cut the right tree. They carried their stone tools and sharpening stones. They carried offerings for the gods.

The most important tool the Hawaiians used was the adze. It had a stone head. The stone head was fastened with sennit to a wooden handle. Adzes were of different sizes. Large ones were used to

chop a tree. Smaller ones were used to cut the branches from a tree. Adzes without handles were used to hollow a tree. All adzes were made of a special kind of hard lava rock. They were carefully shaped. They were ground to a sharp edge.

Men carrying different adzes went to the wet forest. The expert who was their leader chose the tree. He watched the elepaio bird. This bird eats insects and bugs found in rotten wood. If the elepaio pecked at the trunk of a tree, this tree was not chosen. It might look perfect, but if the elepaio was interested in it, the inside of the tree might be rotten.

When the tree had been chosen, the imu was prepared. The food to be offered to the gods was cooked. The eating place was prepared with maile and other vines of the forest. The cooked food was taken from the

ADZES

imu. Part of it was offered, with prayers, to the gods. Then the men sat down to their feast.

After the feast had been eaten, the choppers set to work. They stood around the tall forest tree. They chopped in pairs until the tree fell. Helpers kept them supplied with sharpened adzes.

The men rested after the tree had fallen. While they rested, they watched the elepaio. If an elepaio came and ran along the fallen tree and flew away, the work on that tree was continued. If an elepaio stopped and pecked at the fallen tree, that tree was not made into a canoe. It might not be perfect.

If the experts decided the tree was indeed perfect, the branches were cut from the trunk. The bark was stripped from the trunk. The canoe was marked out. The trunk was partly hollowed. Strips of wood were left to support the seats. These strips were the cleats.

The men stayed in the forest until the canoe was partly finished. When they were ready to take the canoe to the lowlands to be finished, they sent word to their village. Men, women and children came to the forest to help haul the canoe. They brought food for a feast. The food was cooked and eaten.

Ropes were fastened to the front end, or *bow*, of the canoe. Ropes were fastened to the back end, or *stern* of the canoe. The canoe had to be hauled

through the forest. It had to be taken over rocks, and down the sides of valleys. There were no roads in the forests. The Hawaiians had no carts or wagons, because they did not know how to make wheels. Heavy loads had to be dragged or carried.

Men took hold of the canoe ropes. Behind them, women took hold, ready to help haul the canoe. Behind the women, children took hold to help. Everyone helped pull the canoe. Chanters walked beside the people. They sang chants and songs which encouraged everyone to pull carefully and well. Two men helped guide the canoe over the hardest places.

Finally the canoe reached the lowlands. It was hauled into the canoe shed. The canoe shed was like a long house, open at both ends.

Here is part of a Hawaiian poem, which describes canoe building:

"They will hew down the canoe tree until it falls,
      using many adzes,
  Trim off the canoe tree that it might be light,
  Then draw it forth with ropes, tightly held,
  And drag it down to the canoe shed and place it
      within."

CHAPTER TWENTY-THREE

Finishing a Canoe in the Lowlands

WHEN A CANOE had been brought from the forest, it was really only begun. The canoe builders who worked in the canoe shed had a great deal of work to do before the canoe was finished.

The hollowing of the inside was completed; that is, the hull was shaped. The hull was soaked in water. It was dried. It was polished, inside and out. It was painted black.

Holes were drilled near the edge. These holes were made with a tool called a pump drill.

The rim was made and polished. Holes were drilled near the edge of this rim. The holes in the rim matched the holes in the top of the hull. The rim was set in place. It was tied to the hull with ropes of sennit which passed through the holes.

The single canoe, hollowed from one tree, always had an outrigger. Supports to hold the outrigger poles were lashed to the canoe. The outrigger float, and the two curving poles, were tied to-

gether. The ends of the curving poles were lashed
to their supports inside the canoe.

A PUMP DRILL

When the outrigger canoe itself was finished, it
was not ready to use. It had to be supplied with

paddles, a mast for the sails, the sails themselves, an anchor of stone and a bailer of wood or coconut shell.

When the canoe was fitted out, an expert fisherman took it on its first trip. The first fish caught was offered with prayers to the gods. Then the canoe could be used by its owner.

Here is the rest of the poem telling about making a canoe:

"Then hew the canoe, shape the canoe,
  Blacken the canoe, set the cleats,
  Tie the cord to the end of Hakea,
  That is the important cord of the canoe.
  Carry the canoe and drop it in the sea,
  Set up the mast and tie with ropes—
  A rope to the bow, a rope to the stern,
  A rope for packing, a rope for the stay,
  Put on the sails, the bundle of sails,
  At the dawn push off the canoes until they float—
  Push off, sit down, and paddle away."

CHAPTER TWENTY-FOUR

Building a House

HAWAIIAN HOUSES were not all alike. Some were larger than others. Some were more carefully built than others.

The Hawaiian house in the Bishop Museum in Honolulu is a small, well-built house. This is the kind of house described here.

No Hawaiian house had more than one room. A Hawaiian family had several houses, instead of one house with several rooms.

The family had an eating house for the men. It had another for the women, because men and women could not eat together. The family had a sleeping house. Sometimes a family had several other houses.

When a man was going to build a new house, he asked his friends to help him. There were no special house builders. There were, however, some experts who worked so well that they were asked to thatch the roof. Thatching the roof was the most difficult part of the work.

The first thing the house builders needed was heavy wood for the strong posts of the house. These strong posts were set upright, at the corners and along the sides.

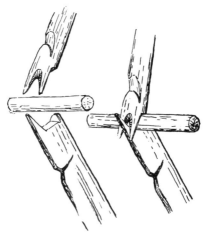

HOUSE POSTS

The large posts of the best houses were naio, kauila, mamane, or kamani wood. Men went to the forests for naio or kauila. They cut mamane or kamani along the beaches. The posts of other houses were ohia lehua wood.

The heavy wood for the large posts was brought to the place where the house was to stand. Men

HAWAIIAN HOUSE

dragged the logs, or carried them on their shoulders.

The posts were trimmed and cut the right length. The top of each was shaped. The picture on page 114 shows how the top of each large post looked when it was finished.

The floor was laid. A good house had a floor of stones and pebbles. You remember when Kawelo was calling to Ma-ka-a-ke-ke, he said, "Leave the pebbles!" He meant, "Get up from your bed on the stone floor."

The helpers took their digging sticks and dug holes for the large posts. They set these posts in place, all around the sides.

They laid long, rather thin posts across the tops of the standing large posts. They tied these together. The Hawaiians had no nails to fasten the pieces of wood together. Sennit was used to tie the timbers of the house together. A great deal of sennit was needed, and some of the helpers were busy making large balls of sennit for the builders to use.

The timbers which would support the roof were cut and trimmed and shaped. These timbers were the *rafters* and *ridge poles*. The rafters and ridge poles were tied to the rest of the framework.

Many short thin sticks were cut. These were tied

PILI GRASS

between the larger timbers of the framework. When these had been tied in place, the framework was finished.

The framework was covered with thatch. *Thatch* is any kind of grass or leaves which is used to cover a house. The Hawaiians used pili grass for the best houses.

Pili grass grows near the sea and also in the uplands. A great deal of it had to be gathered. Piles of it were gathered by the helpers.

Sometimes a house was thatched with banana leaves or hala leaves or sugar cane leaves.

The thatchers took a handful of the thatch. They tied it to the frame. They did this until the entire house, except the opening left for the door, was covered. The Hawaiian house had no windows.

The thatchers left a long piece of thatch hanging over the doorway. This was cut when, after the house had been finished, prayers were offered to the gods.

Here is part of the prayer the owner of the house said before he and his family entered their new house:

> "If a man in trouble enters this house
>   May he be well.
>   If a dying men enters this house,
>   May he be well.
>   Grant life to me,
>   Grant life to my wife,
>   Grant life to my children.
>   Grant life to my relatives,
>   Grant life to my parents,
>   Grant life to my family, those of us on earth."

When the house was finished, the owner provided a feast for all his helpers and other friends and relatives. Mats were spread in the new house. It was decorated with maile, ieie, fern and leis.

When the feast was ready, part of the food was offered, with prayers, to the gods. Here is part of the prayer:

"Here is vegetable food . . .
  And everything else provided for the new
          house . . .
  The house is being offered to you . . .
  Take care of your children
  As the house shelters against the rain,
  The wind, the cold, and the heat of the sun,
  So may the god protect us from misfortunes."

CHAPTER TWENTY-FIVE

Inside the Home

THE HAWAIIAN people used their houses as shelters from the wind and the rain. They lived much more outside than inside their houses.

Because the people lived outdoors more than indoors, they needed few articles of furniture. If you could look inside an old Hawaiian house, you would not think there was any furniture there at all.

In every good Hawaiian house, there were a great many lauhala mats. The floor was covered with them. The bed was made of a pile of these mats.

Women made the mats for the house. They gathered the large leaves of the hala tree. Leaves were gathered as soon as they had dried on the tree, but before they had withered. Leaves gathered at the right time did not have to be prepared immediately for use. They could be left until the matmaker wished to prepare the material.

When the matmaker was ready to work, she first cut off the base of the leaf. She stripped the thorns

MAKING LAUHALA MATS

from the edges of each leaf. She scraped the thorns from the midrib. She flattened each leaf by drawing the hard piece which had been cut from the base down the whole length of the leaf.

The matmaker then rolled the smooth, flat strips over her hand. Nothing more was done for at least twenty-four hours.

After the leaves had been left to flatten for at least a day, the matmaker tore the tough midrib from each leaf and threw it away. She tore the pieces into strips of equal width. She plaited these even strips over and under, over and under, to make a lauhala mat.

Every Hawaiian family had some lauhala mats. Even if the floor was not covered with them, there were several mats in the pile which made the bed.

Other things besides mats were made of lauhala. Inside the sleeping house, there were lauhala pillows. Some baskets were made of lauhala.

The houses of the chiefs often contained very fine mats. These were not made of lauhala. They were made out of the thin stems of the makaloa plant.

Makaloa grew only in damp places. It did not grow on every island. Most of it was found on the island of Niihau.

Makaloa could not be gathered at any time. It

was ready to use for mat-making only once a year. Sometimes not enough could be gathered to make a whole mat. The mat-maker would have to wait for a year for the remainder of the needed material.

These soft mats might have from ten to twenty makaloa stems to the inch. The thin stems were plaited over and under, over and under, in the same way as the wider strips of lauhala were plaited.

Makaloa mats were sometimes hung around the walls to cover the thatch. Sometimes they were used to make the bed soft. They were not used to cover floors.

Hawaiian houses were dark, because they had no windows. Every house had either a lamp or a candle.

LAMPS, CANDLES
AND A TORCH

The lamp was made of stone. It was hollowed out to hold oil. The oil was pressed from kukui nuts. The wick was made of a piece of kapa or lauhala. It was laid in the oil and lighted.

The candle was like a little torch. It was made of a few kukui nuts strung on the tough midrib of a coconut palm leaf. The nuts were so full of oil that they burned slowly when they were lighted.

Hawaiian dishes were made of coconut shell, or wood. Gourds were also used. The Hawaiians did not make dishes out of clay. The dishes were nearly all in the shape of bowls.

Poi bowls were made of coconut shell. Most of the larger bowls or calabashes were made of kou wood, kamani wood or milo wood. Koa wood was never used because this wood has a bitter taste.

Hawaiian wooden bowls were plain. They were hollowed from a single piece of wood. They were carefully made and polished.

Wooden platters, each large enough to hold a roast pig, were often found in the houses of chiefs. These platters were sometimes supported on carved figures.

Gourd calabashes were part of the furniture of the Hawaiian home. They were usually slung in nets and hung up. All sorts of things were kept inside these containers.

Bed covers and clothing were kept in gourd calabashes. The fisherman kept his fishlines and fishhooks in them. Paiai, wrapped in ti leaves, was kept
in such calabashes. Water gourds were hung on a
special stand outside the door.

Inside many houses, you might find a smooth,
round piece of black lava. This was a stone mirror,
or looking-glass.

But you cannot see yourself in a stone! How was
it used? It was placed in the bottom of a calabash
of water. It helped the water to give back a clear
picture, or reflection, of the person looking into the
water.

In rainy or stormy weather, the people brought
everything they used inside the house. You might
find poi boards, digging sticks and adzes in a house.
You might find fish baskets and small nets there.
You might find kapa beaters, olona anvils and poi
pounders there. You might find shell scrapers and
balls of cord there.

Such things were tools, not furniture. We cannot think of the Hawaiian house as furnished. It
did not have to be furnished. Most of the work was
done out of doors. Most of the time was spent out of
doors. The Hawaiian house was a shelter, rather
than a place in which to live and work.

CHAPTER TWENTY-SIX

Making Kapa

THE HAWAIIANS did not need much clothing. The men wore what we call a loin cloth. This was a long, narrow strip passed between the legs. It was knotted to hold it in place. The women wore a short skirt. It was wound about the waist and knotted there. On cool days, both men and women wore shawls over their shoulders.

The loin cloth was called a *malo*. The skirt was called a *pa-u*. The shawl was called a *kihei*.

The malo, the pa-u and the kihei were made of kapa. Bed coverings were made of kapa.

Kapa was made from the inner bark of certain trees and plants. It was made from the inner bark of the mamaki or wauke plants. Sometimes the inner bark of the breadfruit tree was used.

Mamaki grew only in wet highlands. Men climbed from 1500 to 4000 feet in the wet mountains to find mamaki plants.

Wauke could be grown nearer the lowlands. Men often raised wauke. Sometimes a man decided to

126

start a new wauke patch. He looked for a damp, sheltered place. He took shoots from plants which had been cut back and which had grown up again. These were the best shoots for planting.

The wauke planter trimmed the shoots. He left only the leaf bud. He kept the shoots damp over night. He took them to the place which he had chosen. He worked the soil until it was fine and soft. He made a hole for each shoot. Then he planted each shoot. The wauke planter often made shelters of dried banana leaves to protect the young wauke plants.

When the plants had begun to grow, the planter visited the patch and weeded it. He put leaf mold around the plants to help them to grow well. He waited for eighteen months, until the plants were ready to use in making kapa.

When the wauke was ready to use, the plants were cut off near the ground. New plants grew up from the shoots which appeared. The planter kept the patch clear of weeds, so that the plants would grow well.

The men brought bundles of mamaki, or wauke or breadfruit branches to the lowlands. Then the women's work began. Women always made the kapa.

The outer bark was stripped from the branches

and thrown away. The inner bark was soaked for several days, in fresh or salt water.

The strips of bark were taken from the water. They were laid over a stone. They were pounded into thick strips, with a round pounder.

These thick strips were soaked again. They were taken from the water. This time they were laid on a wooden log or anvil.

The kapa anvil was always made of hard wood. It was made of wood which would make a booming sound when the kapa was beaten with wooden beaters. Kawau wood was a favorite wood for the kapa anvil. It grows in dry forests, above a height of 3000 feet. An old song says:

"As the Kawau so is the sound of the ocean."

Women making kapa often struck their booming anvils in such a way as to tell far-away listeners a story. It was always a story of what was happening in their village. Certain strokes stood for words. The far-away kapa makers repeated the story, so that those still farther away could hear it. Sometimes the kapa makers sent a story around an island in a few hours.

The kapa beaters were often made of kauila wood. They had four sides, or faces. Each was carved with a different pattern.

Each side of the beater was first smoothed and

BEATING KAPA

polished. Then it was carved. The carving was done
with a shark's tooth set in a bone handle, or perhaps with a piece of sharp stone. The lines of the

carving were often very close together. They were always very even and carefully made.

The strips of bark were laid on the hard-wood anvils. There they were beaten with the carved wooden beaters. They were beaten together into kapa, the material which the Hawaiians used for cloth.

You remember the prayer of the farmer, when he asked the gods to help him, so that they might "wear bark cloth" with him and his family. He was speaking about kapa, and the plants which furnished the bark used to make kapa.

The bark fibers were beaten into pieces of different sizes and shapes. Long, narrow strips were made for the men's malos. Shorter, wider strips were made for the women's pa-us. Still shorter strips were made for kiheis.

Large sheets were made for bed coverings. Each bed cover was made of four or five sheets, tied together at the corner. The outside sheet was colored. The inner sheets were white.

When the kapa was finished, it was often dyed, and painted or stamped with colored designs. Little paint brushes were made from hala fruit. Stamps were made of bamboo. These stamps had patterns cut into them. They were dipped in colors, and laid on the kapa. Regular designs were thus repeated.

HAWAIIAN KAPA

Here are some of the dyes which the ancient Hawaiians made:

Yellow: Berries of the nau, which grows in both wet and dry forests. Bark and roots of the holei, a tree of the dry districts. Root of the noni.

Red: Berries of the haa. Noni bark. Kou leaves. Leaves of the common fern.

Blue: Leaves and bark of the olapa, a common forest tree. Uki berries.

Black: Bark of the ohia ha, a tree of the wet forests. Leaves of the alahee. Soot of burning kukui nuts.

Brown: Kukui bark.

Kapa was more like paper than cloth. It could not stand much rain. Sometimes it was soaked in kukui nut oil and coconut oil to make it a better protection against the rain.

The Hawaiian protected himself from hard rain by a sort of cape made of ti leaves. You remember the poem, describing the two men in the rainy forests:

"Ti leaf was broken and worn at the back."

Kapa was laid away with sweet-smelling things to perfume it. It was laid in calabashes with maile, mokihana or the powdered heart wood of the sandalwood tree.

CHAPTER TWENTY-SEVEN

Featherwork

IN THE DEEP forests of the Hawaiian Islands lived many different kinds of birds. Some of them were beautiful.

The mamo had a few feathers which were a soft yellow color. The oo also had some beautiful yellow feathers. The iiwi was almost entirely bright red.

Hawaiian chiefs wore feather capes. They wore feather helmets. A *helmet* is a particular kind of head covering. The colored feathers used to make the chiefs' capes and helmets were taken from the forest birds.

Feather gatherers went to the forests. They took some sticky material with them. They put the sticky material along the branches of trees to which they knew the birds would come.

The birds came to the trees. They lighted on the sticky branches. They could not get away.

The men, who had been waiting quietly in the forest, came out. They took hold of each bird. They pulled out the colored feathers. They usually let the birds go free after they had taken the feathers they wished.

132

HAWAIIAN CHIEFS

Feathers, gathered from the forest birds of every district, were brought to the lowlands. They were

tied together into little bunches. These little bunches of feathers were paid as taxes to the chief.

The feather worker made a very fine net of olona for the chief's cape. This net was the size and shape of the finished cape. Sometimes it was wide and long. Sometimes it was short—just long enough to cover the chief's shoulders.

The feather worker covered the net with feathers. He tied each one separately to the fine net. He tied every feather separately, using very fine olona cord. He tied the feathers very close together. No part of the net showed. No piece of the cord showed. The finished cape looked as if it were made of nothing but feathers.

Some capes were all one color. If only one color was used, it was always yellow. Some capes were red and yellow. Others were yellow, black and red. The different colored feathers were put on the net in regular patterns.

Feather helmets were made in different shapes. The helmet maker first made a strong frame of ieie. The frame was the shape and size of the finished helmet. A fine net of olona was fastened to the frame. The feathers which covered the helmet were tied on, just as they were tied to the net of the cape.

No one but a chief could wear a feather cape or a feather helmet.

CHAPTER TWENTY-EIGHT

Hawaiian Life

THE HAWAIIANS did not know about the wheel. They had no wheeled carts of any kind. Men carried heavy loads on their backs. Men dragged heavy logs from the forests.

The Hawaiians had no large animals to help them. The Polynesians, traveling from island group to island group across the Pacific, could not take large animals in their little ships. There were no work animals in the Polynesian islands.

Since the Hawaiians did not have carts nor large animals, they did not need many roads. Men can travel along trails and paths. The Hawaiians made a few stone-paved trails along the shores of different islands.

The Hawaiians made no bridges. Men swam across streams, or used canoes, or waded around cliffs near the shore.

The Hawaiians did not do any loom weaving. They did not know about the loom, on which threads are woven into cloth.

The Hawaiians did not make any pots or dishes of clay. They did not know about pottery making.

The Hawaiians had no iron, except that which floated ashore from some wrecked ship. Such scraps and nails belonged to the chief.

The Hawaiians had no written language. They did not invent any way of writing. Chanters learned the songs and chants which told the people their history. They learned these carefully, and repeated them exactly.

Most children learned the things they needed to know by watching older people and by helping them. Only those young people who were to be certain experts had special training. Special training was given to boys who were to be fishermen or canoe builders. Special training was given to young dancers, chanters, chiefs and priests.

The Hawaiians used wood, stone, bone, shell and plant fibers with great skill. Because all their tools were made of stone, we can say that they lived in the Stone Age.

They were not, however, a true Stone Age people. Their life was very different from that of true Stone Age people.

Hawaiian life, under the chiefs and the law of the land, was ahead of anything known in the Stone Age of man's history. Hawaiian life was not simple,

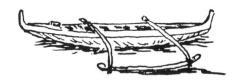

though the materials which the people used were simple.

Hawaiian life was governed by many rules. Even the chiefs obeyed these rules. A chief could make a new rule, but he could not break an old one.

The rules for living were known as the *kapu* system. Kapu means forbidden. The kapu system was made up of rules saying what people could not do; that is, the rules told which things were forbidden.

Men and women were forbidden to eat together. Some foods were forbidden to women. Some foods were forbidden to the common people. It was forbidden to make any sound when the fishermen started out, or when they were lashing their hooks before going fishing.

There were kapu seasons for inshore fishing. There were kapu days when no work might be done.

It was kapu for a common person to come near a chief. It was kapu for a common person to touch a chief's clothing.

It was forbidden for a man from one district to take anything whatever from another district. Men were specially trained to learn and recite the district boundaries, so that no one could make a mistake about his district.

The people learned the proper things to do on every occasion. They knew the prayers and cere-

monies which should be used when a house was dedicated. They knew the right things to do when they planted taro, when they gathered the first leaves of the young taro and when they pulled the first ripe taro. They knew the right things to do when the fisherman started out to fish, and when he returned from fishing.

Hawaiian life was very carefully governed. The people did not do as they wished. They followed the many rules for living. These rules were not simple. Hawaiian life was not the simple life of Stone Age man.

CHAPTER TWENTY-NINE

The Chiefs and the People

MOST OF THE people who lived long ago in Hawaii were not chiefs. Those who were not chiefs were known as common people. The common people lived on the chief's land. During some of their time they worked for the chief.

The people did a good deal of hard work. It was not easy to dig the heavy soil of taro patches. It was not easy to dig ditches and build dams. It was not easy to bring great canoe logs from the mountains.

Long and patient work was required to make a fish net, or a fishline, or a feather cloak. It was hard to cut trees with stone tools, or to hollow bowls and canoes with stone tools, or to shape house timbers.

Huge piles of thatch were collected in order to complete one house. Thousands of feet of cord were twisted to be used in fishing, in building houses and in making canoes. All of these things required long hours of work.

The common people of Hawaii worked long and hard, but they did not work regular hours. They chose their own time for working.

If the day was a good one for a certain kind of fishing, men stopped other things and went fishing. They went on with their other work on another day.

Cooking was hard work, but it was not done regularly. If one family had plenty of cooked food, several other families might join them to eat it. On another day, some one else prepared the imu, and did the hard work.

The people had feasts at the end of a hard piece of work. Sometimes they feasted at the beginning, too.

You remember that when the taro patch soil was prepared, all the people of the village helped. The owner gave a feast for the helpers.

When a house was finished, the owner gave a feast for all the helpers. The hard work of cutting heavy posts, carrying heavy timbers, gathering thatch, twisting cord and thatching the house was forgotten when the house was finished and the feast enjoyed.

Men who went to the forest to cut a canoe tree had a feast before they began their hard work. When it was time to drag the heavy canoe tree to the lowlands, everyone from the village came to the forest to help. Food was brought for a feast. The feast was enjoyed before the hard work began.

The people paid taxes to the chief. Once a year,

they came bringing their taxes. They paid the chief what he asked. He asked for taro, bananas, mats, nets, lines, paddles, kapa, feathers, calabashes and cord. He asked for things which the people made or raised.

After the people had paid their taxes, the Makahiki began. This was the season of sports and games. All work was stopped while the people took part in the sports and games of the season. In old Hawaii, hard work was usually followed by some celebration which the people enjoyed.

There was a difference, however, between the life of the chiefs and the life of the common people. The chiefs had the best houses. They had the finest mats. They had the largest and best canoes. They had the best food. They were the only ones who could wear feather cloaks and helmets.

All these things were not enough. An old Hawaiian song says:

"Thou art satisfied with food, O thou common man!
To be satisfied with lands is for the chief."

This means that most of the people, the common people, wished only for enough food. The chief wanted more than this. He wanted much land, so that he would have many people to work for him.

The common people were proud of their chief. They were proud of their chief's strength. They were proud when they listened to the long chants which told about their chief.

Each chief had name songs which told about him and his family. Here is part of one of the songs about Kamehameha I, the greatest chief of all. He was the first king of all the islands.

"To the chief belongs the whole land!
To the chief belong the ocean and the land!
The night is his.   The day is his.
For him are the seasons—the winter, the summer,
The months, and the seven stars of heaven . . .
Everything belongs to the chief . . .
All things that float ashore, the bird driven upon
   the land,
The thick-shelled broad-backed turtle, the dead
   whales,
The yearly uhu of the sea.
Let the chief live forever!   Evermore a chief!
Let him be borne forth gloriously with the long
   gods and the short gods!
Let him go forth fearlessly, the chief holding the
   island!"

APPENDIX A

Additional Hawaiian Poetry

Arise, Kona, land of the calm seas!
. . . Make a move, Kohala, arise!
Make a move, Kohala, thou of the solid step . . .
Arise, Hilo!
Hilo of the steady rain of the sharp head . . .
Arise, Puna!
Puna, the land made fragrant by the hala
From one end to the other,
To the very breadfruit trees of Kailua,
That stand untouched by the winds of Kau.
Arise, Kau!
Kau, the large windy land,
Land where the current draws down to Alae,
Where the canoes sail here and there.

———

That is Hilo!   That is Hilo!
That is Hilo of the incessant rains,
The increasing rains,
The ceaseless rains of Hilo.
That is Hamakua of the steep cliffs . . .

143

OF THE HILO RAIN

Hilo . . . swims in the ocean . . .
And the village rests in the bowl,
Its border surrounded with rain.
Sharp from the sky the tooth of Hilo's rain!
Trenched is the land, scooped out by the downpour—
Tossed and like gnawing surf is Hilo's rain . . .
The flood waters pour in Wailuku;
Swollen is Waiau, flooding the point Makupane;
And red leap the waters of Anuenue.
A roar to heaven sends up Kolopule,
Shaking like thunder, mist rising like smoke.
The rain cloud unfurls in the heavens;
Dark grows Hilo, black with the rain.
The skin of Hilo grows rough from the cold;
The storm cloud hangs low o'er the land.

OF THE RAIN OF THE WINDWARD DISTRICTS

'Twas in Koolau I met with the rain;
It comes with the lifting and tossing of dust,
Advancing in columns, dashing along,
The rain, it sighs in the forest . . .
It smites, it smites now the land . . .
Full run the streams, a rushing flood;
The mountain walls leap with the rain.

OF PANAEWA FOREST

In the heart of Panaewa
Lehuas were heavy with bud.

OF FOREST RAIN

Panaewa's rain beats down the lehuas,
A rain by the sea smites the halas of Puna.

OF VALLEYS

As I traveled above Waipio
Mine eyes drank in that valley.

OF THE SURF

The surf-spraying wind of Waialua
Carries the spray of the surf high,
Even to the mountain top.

OF THE SURF-RIDER

Let the sun guide the board Halepo,
Till Halepo lifts on the swell.
It mounts the swell that rolls from Kahiki . . .
The roller plumes and ruffles its crest.

Here comes the champion surf-man,
While wave-ridden wave beats the island,
A fringe of mountain-high waves . . .
A surf this to ride at noontide . . .
Glossy the skin of the surf-man;
Undrenched the skin of the expert;
Wave-feathers fan the wave-rider . . .
You've seen the grand surf of Puna, of Hilo.

OF WAVES

Roll on, oh wave, up to the beach
To the pohuehue vines.
You cannot, you cannot reach
The coconut trees of Kane.

OF THE STORM AT SEA

Gently! Gently! Gently!
Come the rain, the wind, the storm . . .
Get up from your seats,
Take out your paddles,
Pull up the weight.
Watch for the waves
As they twist and rise,
As the waves twist and beat

On the outside of the canoe.

The wave is become quiet at the bow.

Swing the canoe around and let the wave pass between . . .

The waves will perhaps open up my canoe.

It will swamp.

Because of the swamping of the small canoe,

The large canoe will also swamp.

Bind the paddles together,

For they will be the only burden of the swamped
canoe.

The small paddle, the large paddle,

The long paddle, the short paddle,

The small bailing cup, the large bailing cup,

The coarse bailing cup, the thin bailing cup,

After rescuing several things from the swamped
canoe

Comes the thought to float the canoe . . .

This rope is drawn, that rope is drawn;

Some will rush here, some will rush there.

The large wave will rise,

The small wave will break,

The sticks at the bow will fly off,

The sticks at the stern will fly off . . .

Had the sailing-master seen the star

You would have reached land.

OF STARTING OUT IN A CANOE

Lift up the canoe,
Get aboard, paddle away, get on.
Let the people get aboard
With the sounding sticks,
With the binding ropes,
With the floaters.
The canoe-master is aboard.

OF THE HOUSE

There Hilo is thatching,
Finishing, ridging,
Trimming until satisfactory,
Rounding off, boards standing,
Boards stood up and cut.
For the house there is spreading of the grass,
Unfolding and spreading of the mat,
Covering over with bed clothes,
And using of pillows.   There is sleeping,
Awaking, standing up and walking about.
There is preparation of food;
The fish and the water; there is eating.
There is an end to the eating,
There is washing of the hands,
And there is a coming out.

OF LEIS

At Waiakea, in Hilo
They rise early in the morning
To weave fresh wreaths of lehua.

————

Kapo came down to earth,
Kapo saw the lehua,
Kapo broke the lehua,
Kapo bundled the lehua,
Kapo plucked the lehua,
Kapo strung the lehua,
Kapo braided the lehua,
Kapo wore a lei of lehua.

————

Kapo came down to earth.
Kapo saw the maile,
Kapo broke the maile,
Kapo bundled the maile,
Kapo stripped the maile,
Kapo tied the maile,
Kapo twisted the maile,
Kapo wore a lei of maile.

OF KAUAI AND OAHU

Kauai, my beloved,
Green are thy banks of flowers,
Flanked by the hau blossoms at Wailua.

Beautiful is Waialeale in the sky.
Sea waves absorb many waters.

. . . A cluster of islands floating in the sea . . .
Kauai, great and peaceful,
That is under the lee of Waianae.
Kaena is a cape . . .
Kaala is a mountain ridge covered with dew,
And Waialua is situated below, O Waialua . . .
The tail of the white shark is Kaena,
The shark stretching away towards Kauai.
Below is Kauai, my land,
O great Kauai, island filled with lehua.

Hawaiian Legends, for Reading and Dramatizing

A LEGEND is an old story, so old that no one knows who first told it. No one knows how much the legend has changed since it was first told.

Here are a few Hawaiian legends. You may enjoy reading them. You may enjoy dramatizing them. You may enjoy painting pictures to illustrate them. They are Hawaiian stories of long ago.

HOW THE SKY WAS PUT IN PLACE

A very long time ago, the sky almost touched the land. The trees were pressed down, so that their leaves were flat. No one could see the hills and mountains. The Sun was so close to the earth that fields were burned by its rays. People were very uncomfortable.

Maui was the son of the goddess Hina and the god Ku. He looked at the sky pressing down on the islands of Hawaii. He looked at the burned fields. He looked at the uncomfortable people. He decided to lift the sky.

151

Maui put his shoulders under the sky. He gave one great lift. The sky was lifted to the tree tops. The trees stood and stretched. They waved their branches. But all their leaves stayed flat. They had been pressed down so long that they could not change. That is why the leaves of the trees are flat today.

Maui gave another lift. The sky rose to the mountain tops. For the first time, the people saw the mountains of their islands.

Maui lifted once more. This time the sky went much higher. It went to the place where you see it today.

After Maui had done this, the Sun was far away. Its hot rays did not burn the fields. The people were more comfortable and happy than they had been.

WHY HAWAII HAS LONG DAYS OF SUNSHINE

After Maui had lifted the sky and put it in its place, there was not quite enough sunshine in Hawaii. The Sun hurried across the sky. It was dark before the people could finish their work.

Maui's mother Hina, who lived under Rainbow Falls near Hilo, made kapa all day long. When the Sun had set, the kapa was finished, but it was no

dry. There was never enough sunshine to dry it.

Hina said she wished the Sun would shine just a little longer each day, so that her kapa could dry. Maui made a plan to help her.

Maui twisted some long, strong cord. He made several nooses in the ends of his cord. He changed his shape. He followed the Sun to its home on the top of Haleakala. Haleakala means "house of the Sun." The Sun slept there every night.

Maui hid behind a rock near the top of Haleakala. He fastened one end of his rope to a strong tree there. He waited for the Sun to wake up.

At dawn, the Sun stretched one long leg, or ray, over the edge of the mountain. Maui threw his rope and caught the Sun by one leg. He caught each leg of the Sun as it came over the edge of the mountain.

The Sun could not move. It pulled and pulled, but the strong ropes which were fastened to the tree held it.

"Let me go!" said the Sun.

"I will let you go," said Maui, "if you will promise to go more slowly every day. Hina needs more sunshine to dry her kapa. The people need longer days so that they can finish their work."

"No!" said the Sun. The Sun pulled again, but it could not get away.

The Sun finally promised what Maui asked. It

promised to go more slowly across the sky every day. It promised not to shine too hot upon the fields It promised not to burn the young taro plants with its hot rays.

That is why Hawaii has long days of sunshine That is why the Sun does not shine too hot upon the fields of Hawaii.

HOW THE SECRET OF FIRE–MAKING WAS DISCOVERED

Long, long ago, when Maui and his mother Hina and his brothers lived in Hawaii, no one knew how to make fire. The people ate all their food raw.

Maui and his brothers went fishing every day Every day, when they were out fishing in their canoe, they saw smoke rising. It rose from one of the Halai hills behind Hilo. Every day, Maui and his brothers hurried back to land. They ran to the Halai hills. They found nothing but ashes. They saw nothing but a few alae birds flying away.

One day, Maui heard the alae birds talking. "We cannot have a fire today," they said, "because Maui has not gone fishing. We must wait until tomorrow when Maui will be away."

Maui had done so many wonderful things that the alae birds were afraid he would find out their

secret. When Maui heard what the birds said, he made a plan.

Maui told his brothers to take a big calabash with them when they went fishing the next day. He told them to put it in the canoe so that the birds would think Maui was there in the canoe with them. His brothers did as he said.

Maui went secretly to the Halai hills. He hid in the bushes. He watched the alae birds come. He saw the smoke of their fires. But he was not near enough to see how they made fire.

Maui jumped out of the bushes. He ran to grab one of the burning sticks. The alae birds quickly put out every single stick. They flew away, all but one bird. Maui caught this bird.

"Tell me how you make fire," said Maui, "or I will kill you."

"If you kill me," said the alae bird, "how can you learn the secret?"

"Tell me!" said Maui.

"No!" said the alae bird.

"Tell me!" said Maui.

"Rub a stick and a banana leaf together," said the bird, finally.

Maui found a stick. Maui found a banana leaf. He held the bird with one hand. With the other, he

rubbed the stick and the banana leaf together for a long time. No fire came.

"That is not the secret," said Maui. "Tell me the truth."

"Rub a taro stalk and a stick together," said the bird.

Maui found a taro stalk. Maui found a stick. Maui rubbed the taro stalk for a long time. He made a deep groove in the taro stalk. (That is why every taro stalk today has a deep groove.) But Maui could not make fire this way.

Maui was angry. "I'll rub your head with this stick, if you do not tell me the truth," he said.

Maui rubbed the alae bird's head. The feathers on the top of the alae bird's head grew red with blood. (After that, every alae bird had red feathers on its head.)

The alae bird spoke. "Rub a dry branch of hau with a hard stick," it said.

Maui got a dry branch of hau. Maui got a hard stick. He rubbed them together, and fire came!

Maui let the alae bird go. He told all the people how to make fire. After that, the people of Hawaii had cooked food to eat.

THE ISLAND AT THE MOUTH OF THE WAILUKU RIVER IN HILO

Long, long ago, when Hina and her son Maui were living on the island of Hawaii, a wicked dragon lived there, too. He hated Maui and Hina. He was afraid of Maui because Maui was good. The dragon made a plan to kill Hina first.

Hina used to make kapa in a cave far up the Wailuku River in Hilo. One day, when Maui was away from home, she went to this cave. Moo Kuna, the wicked dragon, thought this was his chance to kill Hina.

Moo Kuna made a high dam of rocks across the Wailuku River below the cave. The river water could not go over the high dam. It formed a deep pool above the dam.

The river water kept flowing down into the pool. The pool rose higher and higher. It grew deeper and deeper. The pool reached to the cave.

Hina and her women looked out. All about them was deep water. The river banks were covered. The water was rising higher and higher. It would soon go into the cave. They would drown, because there was no way to get out.

Hina called for help. No one answered her. Far

away, on the island of Maui, Hina's son Maui felt that something was happening to his mother. He jumped into his magic canoe. With three strokes of the paddle, he reached the shores of Hawaii.

The minute Maui landed, he saw that the mouth of the Wailuku River was dry. Such a thing had never happened before. Maui hurried up the dry river bed.

Maui reached the deep pool. He heard his mother calling from the cave. The deep waters were going into the cave.

Maui had no time to tear down the high dam. Quickly he dug his kauila club into the river bed. He made great holes there. The water in the pool flowed away into the holes which Maui had made.

The women came out. They were safe.

Moo Kuna was frightened. He swam down the river as fast as he could. Maui heated stones. He threw the hot stones into the deep holes he had made in the river bed. The water in the holes boiled. These holes are the Boiling Pots which you can see today.

Moo Kuna came swimming down the river. He reached the Boiling Pots. The hot water burned him. He swam on. The hot water in the next Boiling Pot burned him. At the river's mouth, Moo Kuna, the wicked dragon, died.

Moo Kuna lies there at the mouth of the Wailuku River today. He is an island of stone, the black rock island of Moo Kuna.

THE RAINBOW

Hawaii is a land of many rainbows. Rainbows are seen when the sun shines through mist or rain. Sometimes they are seen over the ocean, when a light rain has swept down some valley and out to sea. They are most often seen in the valleys.

The Hawaiians did not know the cause of rainbows. Hawaiian legends say that rainbows followed certain chiefs, or certain gods as they walked about over the islands. There are many legends about the rainbow. Here is one of them:

Long, long ago, a great chief lived on the very top of Kaala Mountain in the Waianae Range of Oahu. He had twin children, a boy and a girl. Their mother died when they were born.

The chief had to go away from home for a long time. His children were not happy at home without him. They ran away.

They were children of the mountain mists, and children of a very great chief. Wherever they went, rainbows followed them.

The children went first to Nuuanu Valley in

Honolulu. Rainbows stood over their hiding place. Everyone knew where they were. They ran on still farther. They did not wish to be taken home.

The children went to the hill behind Punahou, at the entrance to Manoa Valley. They hid under a rock.

These children of the wet mountains wished for a pool of clear, fresh water to swim in. They missed their cool mountain home. A friendly water god said he would give them fresh water.

The water god made Punahou Spring for the children. He told them the water in the spring would flow forever. The children swam and played in the cool spring water.

The moment they came out into the valley, rainbows stood over Manoa Valley. Everyone knew the children were there.

By this time, their father had returned home. "Where are my children?" he asked. He soon learned that they had run away because they were not happy without him.

Their father went to look for them. He saw the rainbows over Manoa Valley. He knew his children were there. He went for them, and took them home to live.

The children were glad to go home with their father. Sometimes, however, they wished to look

again at the spring which they had loved. They came back often to look at Punahou Spring. Every time they came, rainbows stood over Manoa Valley.

Every time you see a rainbow over Manoa Valley, you may think of these children of the old legend. You will know that they are looking once more at Punahou Spring.

THE TARO PATCHES OF KAU

Long, long ago, there were two taro plants living in Kona on Hawaii. They were large, beautiful plants. They belonged to a chief.

One day, the chief was going to have a feast. He told his men to gather the large taro. The two taro plants heard this. They did not wish to be eaten. In the night, they moved to the other side of the taro patch. When the men came to gather them, they could not be found.

The chief went to look for his two fine taro plants. He found them, and sent men to get them. The plants moved in the night. The men could not find them. This happened many times. The chief became very angry with the two plants.

The plants were afraid, and decided to move farther away. In the night, they took wings and flew to another taro patch. The chief followed them.

Everyone in Kona was talking about the two taro plants which did not wish to be eaten.

The taro plants flew and flew. The chief followed them everywhere. The plants grew tired. They fell to the ground. The chief stopped when he saw the plants fall. He told his men to get the imu ready to cook the taro.

While the imu was being prepared, the taro plants rested. They were rested enough to fly away again. They were gone when the men went to take them for the imu.

At last, a strong wind blew them into Kau. The chief could not follow them there. They lived there for many years. They had many children. That was why there were once many taro patches in Kau.

WHY THE OWL WAS SACRED

Long, long ago, there was a man named Kapoi. He lived in Honolulu, on the slopes of Punchbowl Hill. His thatched roof needed mending. One day, he went to Kewalo for new thatch.

Kapoi gathered the thatch near the shore at Kewalo. On his way home, he rested in the shade of a large tree. As he lay there resting, he looked up. He saw a bird's nest.

Kapoi climbed the tree. He looked in the nest.

There were seven eggs there, just the thing for his supper, he thought. He gathered the eggs and carried them home.

Kapoi built a fire. He was preparing to roast the eggs for his supper. As he was about to cook the eggs, he heard a voice calling him.

"Kapoi, Kapoi, give me back my eggs!" said the voice.

Kapoi looked up and saw an owl. "I gathered these eggs," said Kapoi. "They are mine. I am going to eat them for my supper."

The owl called again. "Kapoi, Kapoi, please give me back my eggs. They are my eggs, not yours."

Kapoi felt sorry for the owl. He gave the eggs back. The owl thanked him, and told him to build a little temple there.

Now Kapoi was not a chief. He was a common man. No common man could build a temple. Kapoi, however, built the temple where the owl had told him to build it.

The chief of Oahu heard about Kapoi's temple. He was very angry. It was against the law for a common man to build a temple. He sent his men to take Kapoi. He told his men to bring Kapoi to him.

Kapoi was brought before the chief. The chief told him he must die, because he had broken the law.

The owls of every island heard that Kapoi must die. Owls came to Oahu from Niihau, from Kauai, from Molokai, from Lanai, from Kahoolawe, from Maui and from Hawaii. The Oahu owls joined them. Every owl in the islands came to save Kapoi.

The owls fought against the chief and his men. The owls would not let the chief kill Kapoi. The chief saw that he must forgive Kapoi. The owls had never fought for a common man, nor for any man, before.

The chief forgave Kapoi. The chief made the owl a sacred bird. From that time, the owl was a sacred bird, and all Hawaiians knew it.

LAKA'S CANOE

Laka was a young boy. He wished to make a canoe. His grandmother told him to go to the forests with his adze. She told him to find a tall tree with a leaf shaped like a new moon. She told him to cut this tree.

If you look at a koa leaf, you will see that it is shaped like a new moon. Laka's grandmother was telling him to find the right kind of canoe tree, a koa tree.

Laka went to the wet forest with his adze. He found the right tree, a tall tree with a leaf like a new

moon. He worked hard. He chopped down the tree. He went home to rest that night.

The next day he went to the forest to work on his canoe. No tree was cut. Laka found another tall tree with a leaf like a new moon. He cut this tree. He went home to rest.

The next day, he went back to work on his canoe. No tree was cut. This happened several times. Laka was tired and angry.

Finally, he dug a deep ditch where the tree would fall. He cut another tree. It fell into the ditch. Laka did not go home that night. He hid in the ditch beside the canoe tree. He watched to see what would happen.

In the night, he heard a great humming sound. He peeped out. Hundreds of little men were standing beside Laka's canoe tree. "Let us put this tree back, the way we have all the others," said the little men.

They all took hold of the tree. They began to lift it out of the ditch. Laka jumped out of the ditch. He grabbed one of the little men.

"Have you been doing this every night?" he asked angrily. "I shall kill you for this."

"Oh, Laka, do not kill any of us," said the little men. "If you will promise not to kill us, we will make your canoe for you. You need do only two

things—make a canoe shed for your canoe, and give us some food for working for you."

Laka looked at the little men. Now he knew they were menehune, the little men who could do anything, and do it in one night. He promised to do what they said.

Laka went home. He built a canoe shed. He prepared food for the menehune. He prepared a shrimp for each one of the little men.

Before dawn, Laka heard the humming sound again. With the first hum, the little men lifted the canoe. With the second, they carried it on their hands. They did not drag it. They carried it into the canoe shed.

Laka gave each one of the menehune a whole shrimp. They were very much pleased. They ate the food. Then they went home. Laka's canoe was finished.

OLA'S DITCH

Ola was the high chief of Kauai. The people of Waimea on Kauai had no water. Their fields were drying because there was no water.

The chief thought of the menehune. They could help the people. Only the menehune could build a dam and a new ditch in one night, and get water quickly.

Ola sent a man to ask the help of the menehune. Ola ordered food prepared to feed the little men. Ola told everyone to go quietly into his sleeping house, and wait for help.

In the night, hundreds of little men came from their homes in the Kauai mountains. Each one carried a large stone. Each little man put his large stone into place across the river. Each stone fitted. The dam was finished.

Quickly the little men dug the long new ditch from the pool above the dam. They made the walls of stone. They finished the stone walls of the long new ditch. Water flowed from the pool into the taro patches of the flat land at Waimea.

The little men sat down to the feast prepared for them. They ate their feast. Before dawn, they had gone back to their home in the Kauai mountains.

The menehune ditch may still be seen. Its name is Kiki-a-ola, or Ola's Water Way.

THE BUNDLED SPRING

Near Waialua on Oahu is a spring whose Hawaiian name is Kawaipuolo. This means bundled spring. This is how the spring got its name:

Long, long ago, the people of Waialua had to go to a spring in the mountains to get water. They

wished for water nearer their taro patches. They asked the menehune to help them.

One night, the menehune went to the mountain spring. They picked it up from its rock bed. They wrapped it in a bundle of ti leaves. They carried the bundled spring to the lowlands.

They set the spring in place near Waialua. In the morning, there was the new spring, with its stream of fresh water. The people named it Kawaipuolo because the menehune had brought it in a bundle from the mountains.

THE SPEAR OF KAPUNOHU

Kapunohu was a chief of Kohala. He was strong and powerful. He had a great spear. One day, he threw his spear through a row of 800 trees. The spear went through every one of the trees.

Kapunohu's spear went so fast that the sugar cane over which it passed rustled. The blades of grass were moved, and clouds of dust arose when Kapunohu's spear passed over the ground.

Kapunohu went to the other islands. Everywhere he showed how far he could throw his spear.

Kapunohu came to Kauai. He stopped at Lawai in Koloa. At that time, a chief of Kauai was known for his skill in casting a stone with a sling. He could

cast a stone for five miles. Everyone on Kauai was afraid of this chief. No one would travel between Koloa and Nawiliwili for fear of the chief who lived there.

Kapunohu started off from Koloa. The people begged him not to go, because of the Kauai chief. Kapunohu said that in his land, Kohala, on the island of Hawaii, only children used slings. They were children's toys, he said, and he was not afraid.

The chief of Kauai heard what Kapunohu had said. He was angry. He said they would see who could send his weapon the farthest. Everyone came to see the test.

The chief of Kauai threw the stone from his sling. It went from Koloa six miles to Anahola.

Kapunohu took his spear. He threw it from Koloa. It went to the Wailua River. It passed through the river waters. It went on to Anahola. It went through the ridge of the mountain behind Anahola. It made a hole in the mountain ridge which may still be seen. The spear went on. It went on and on, to Hanalei. There it stopped.

Kapunohu had won the test. Kapunohu became the chief of Kauai.

THE KING'S RIDDLES

Long, long ago, there was a King of Kauai who was very skillful in three things. He could throw a spear very skillfully. He could box. He could make riddles which few could answer.

One day a stranger named Paka came to Kauai. He wanted something the King had. He knew that the only way to get it would be to beat the King at spear throwing and at boxing. He must also be able to answer the King's riddles. Then he could ask anything he wished, and the King must give it to him.

The King came out. He had his spear with him.

"Who will throw first?" asked the King.

"You may throw your spear first," said Paka.

Paka did not know whether the King would throw the spear in one direction or the other. He did not know whether the King would throw the spear at him, or at a mark far away.

The King threw his spear. He threw it at Paka. Paka caught the spear between his arm and his side. He held it there. Then he let it drop.

The King was surprised. He waited for Paka to throw his spear. But Paka stood still. The King went away. The King had not beaten Paka at spear throwing.

The next day, the King and his men were boxing. "Let the stranger box with me," said the King.

The King threw Paka. Paka rose, and threw the King. The King lay on the ground a long time without moving. Paka had beaten the King at boxing.

The next day the King sent for his runner. "Go around the whole island," said the King, "and tell every person on Kauai to come to answer my riddles tomorrow. Everyone must come."

The runner started out. The runner had never been given good food to eat. The runner had never been given new clothes to wear. The runner was thin, dirty and in rags. No one had ever been kind to him.

The runner called to all the people on the island. He told them the King's wish.

The runner came to the place where Paka was staying. Paka looked out, and saw the thin, hungry man in rags. "Bring that man in," said Paka to his men, "and wash him. Give him new clothes, and give him some good food."

Paka's men did as Paka told them.

"This is the first time," said the King's runner, "that anyone has given me good food, or been kind to me. Now I shall do something for you," said he.

"What can you do for me?" asked Paka. Paka

was a great chief on his own island. He did not know what the poor runner could do for him.

"I can tell you the answer to the King's riddles," said the runner. "Tomorrow, if you do not give the right answers, the King is going to have you killed. I can save your life with these answers."

"Tell me," said Paka.

"This is the first riddle," said the runner.

"Put it all around from top to bottom,
  Leave, and leave a place with nothing around."

And he whispered the answer to Paka. (Do you know the answer?)

"This is the second riddle," said the runner.

"The men that stand up
The men that lie down
The men that are folded."

And he whispered the answer to Paka. (Do you know the answer?)

The next day, every man, woman and child on the island of Kauai came to hear the King's riddles.

The King stood up. "Let the stranger answer first," he said. He looked at Paka. He told the first riddle:

"Put it all around from top to bottom,
  Leave, and leave a place with nothing around."

Everyone waited for Paka to speak. Paka spoke slowly.

"The answer is *house*. The answer is house because a house is thatched all around from top to bottom, and only the door is left with nothing."

"That is the right answer," said the King. "This is the second riddle:

> "The men that stand up
> The men that lie down
> The men that are folded."

Everyone waited for Paka to speak. Paka answered, "The answer is *house*. The men that stand up are the large posts. The men that lie down are the smaller posts. The men that are folded are the bundles of thatch."

"Yes, that is the right answer," said the King. He was surprised that he could not beat the stranger in spear throwing, or in boxing. He was surprised that the stranger could answer his riddles.

"Now," said Paka, "You must give me what I ask." The King agreed. That was the rule.

Paka asked for the most beautiful girl in the King's house. He wished to marry her and take her home to his island to live.

The King agreed. Paka and his beautiful wife left for their home on another island.

THE SHELLS OF KEAAU

At Keaau, in Puna, lived a common man whose name was also Keaau. He had two magic shells. He took them with him when he went fishing. All he did was show the shells. When lobsters saw the magic shells, they left the sea and climbed into Keaau's canoe.

Umi, the high chief of Hawaii, heard about Keaau's wonderful shells. He wanted them. Since he was the high chief, he could ask for anything he wanted. He sent some men to ask for Keaau's shells. Keaau had to give the shells to Umi's men.

Keaau was very unhappy without his shells. He wanted to get them back. He could not ask for the shells. He thought that if he could find the right man to help him, he might be able to get them back secretly.

Keaau went to different islands, looking for the right man to help him. Near Mokapu, on the island of Oahu, he found a man named Iwa. Iwa said he thought he could get the shells back secretly.

Iwa went with Keaau to the island of Hawaii. They paddled along the shores of Hawaii. They saw Umi out fishing, near Kailua. They were sure he had the magic shells with him.

Iwa told Keaau to hold the canoe where it was.

He told Keaau not to show himself, and to wait for him to return. Iwa then dived to the bottom of the deep waters off Kailua.

Iwa, who was a very fine diver, walked along the bottom of the sea. He walked until he came to the place where Umi's canoe was. He swam upward, almost to the surface.

Iwa saw the magic shells. They were fastened to Umi's line. Iwa unfastened the shells. He dived down with the line, and fastened it to some rocks at the bottom of the sea. He swam back to Keaau's canoe. He gave Keaau the shells. Keaau paddled back to his home in Puna. Iwa swam to the Kona shore.

Keaau, in Puna, went fishing with his shells again. Again the lobsters climbed into his canoe.

Umi sat all day long in his canoe off the Kona coast. He began to pull his line in, but it did not come. Umi was afraid to pull it very hard, for fear he would break the magic shells.

Umi stayed in his canoe several days. He sent his divers down to see what had happened to his line. None of Umi's divers could go deep enough to find out.

Umi sent some men to shore to get the finest divers. Runners went around Hawaii, calling for the best divers to go down for the king.

While the runners were going all around Hawaii, they happened to meet Iwa. Iwa told them that there was no use to dive for the shells. He told them the shells were gone, and that the line was fastened to a rock at the bottom of the sea.

Umi sent for Iwa when he heard this.

"Can you get the shells for me?" asked Umi.

"Yes, I can get them for you," said Iwa.

Iwa went to Keaau's home in Puna. He watched Keaau. He saw Keaau put the magic shells in a secret place under the roof thatch of his house.

In the night, Iwa went softly into Keaau's house. He took the magic shells. He took them to Umi, the high chief.

Keaau never got his shells back. In those days, everything belonged to the high chief.

THE MAGIC FISHHOOK OF PEARL

Long, long ago, there was a common man named Kuula. A sea bird gave him a magic fishhook of pearl. You remember that the aku fishermen used pearl fishhooks when they went out alone for aku.

Kuula used the magic fishhook. He always caught many aku. He always gave some to his friend the sea bird.

One day, the high chief went fishing for aku. Kuula went out the same day. Kuula caught many aku. The high chief caught none.

In those days, everything belonged to the chief. The high chief asked for Kuula's fishhook. Kuula had to give it to him.

Kuula caught no more aku. Soon he had nothing to eat. His friend the sea bird had nothing to eat. His wife had nothing to eat. His children had nothing to eat.

Kuula and his wife put their baby son Aiai near a stream. It was near a place where the high chief's daughter often went swimming. The high chief's daughter found the little boy. She took him home with her.

Aiai lived in the high chief's house. When he grew up, he married the high chief's daughter.

Aiai's wife asked him to get some aku for her. Aiai said, "I cannot go aku fishing unless I have a canoe and a pearl fishhook."

Aiai's wife went to her father. She asked him to give her husband a canoe and a pearl fishhook, so he could catch aku for her.

The high chief said, "Your husband may take a

canoe from the canoe shed. And here is a pearl fishhook for him to use."

Aiai had learned the story of the magic fishhook
which the chief had taken from his own father. He
thought this was the fishhook. He took a canoe from
the canoe shed. He took the fishhook. He went out
for aku.

As soon as he had gone fishing, a sea bird came
and watched him. Aiai was sure this was the sea
bird which was his father's friend.

Aiai threw the pearl fishhook out over the sea.
He skimmed the shining hook over the surface of
the sea. Not one aku came. Not one aku followed
the shining hook.

Aiai came back to shore.

"Where is the aku?" asked his wife.

"I could not catch any aku," said Aiai. "Perhaps
this fishhook is no good. Perhaps your father has
another fishhook of pearl for me to use."

The chief's daughter went to ask her father if he
had another pearl fishhook. He did not remember
that he had another.

"Let us look," said the chief's daughter. "Let us
look through all your calabashes and see if we can
find one."

The chief looked through all his calabashes. He
took out the fishlines in the calabashes. He took out

the strong fishhooks and the little fishhooks, stored in the calabashes. Finally, down in the bottom of the last calabash, he found another pearl fishhook.

The chief gave this fishhook to his daughter to take to her husband. Aiai went out again for aku.

The sea bird came and watched Aiai. Aiai threw the line. He skimmed the shining fishhook over the water. Hundreds of aku came. They jumped into the canoe. The canoe was filled with aku. The sea bird ate all the aku he wished. The canoe was still full of fish.

The sea bird took the magic hook and flew away with it. Every day, the sea bird brought the hook to Aiai. The sea bird never gave it again to any fisherman to keep. He let only Kuula and Aiai use the magic hook of shining pearl.

Even the chief could not get the magic hook again. He had no power over the sea bird.

THE RAIN TEMPLE

Long, long ago, a woman who lived on Molokai made kapa every day. Every day, her brothers teased her. They sent rain to fall on the kapa which was spread out to dry.

This happened many times. The kapa was never finished, because it never dried.

One day, the woman thought of a plan. She built a stone temple near the place where she made kapa. When the rain drops came, she caught them in the hot stones of the temple. The rain drops were cooked in the hot stones.

No rain was left to fall upon the drying kapa. After that, the woman always finished making her kapa.

The rain temple, whose Hawaiian name is Ka-imu-kalua-ua, still stands on Molokai. You can see it if you look for it.

THE ROUGH LAVA FLOW OF KAPOHO

Lava rocks are of many different shapes. Sometimes the rocks are very large. Sometimes they are smooth. Sometimes they are rough.

The Hawaiians had many stories about different lava rocks and lava flows. Here is one of them.

Long, long ago, there was a chief of Kauai. He was a great holua racer. The holua was a sled. Holua racers took their sleds to steep slopes. They threw themselves on the sleds and slid down the steep slopes.

The chief of Kauai, who was a very good holua racer, heard of a good holua racer on the island of

Hawaii. With his family, and many of his household possessions, he sailed for the island of Hawaii, to race.

The chief landed in Puna, near Kapoho. His family came on shore. Many people gathered to see the famous holua racer of Kauai.

The chief went out to slide. He took his sled. His brother went with him. He also took his sled. They were going to try the slopes of Hawaii.

The brothers were just about to start, when they saw an old woman standing there. She asked the chief for his sled. He looked at her, and said, "No!"

The old woman asked for the chief's brother's sled. The chief's brother did not like to say No, so he let the old woman take his sled.

The old woman went down the steep slope. She did not go very far, nor very fast, and everyone laughed.

The old woman came back to the top of the slide. Again she asked the chief for his sled. Again he said "No!" He started down the slide.

The chief heard a noise behind him. He looked back. There was no old woman there! There was a young and angry woman, coming quickly. Fire and smoke came with her! Lava flowed with her!

The chief knew that this was Pele, the Volcano Goddess. She had pretended to be an old woman.

He had been rude to her, and she was coming with her volcano fires to catch him!

The chief went faster and faster down the slide. Pele followed still faster after him. The fires of Pele, the lava rocks of Pele, went over all the people gathered to see the holua race.

The chief's family was covered with lava. The chief's possessions were covered. All the people were covered under the lava rocks of Pele.

No one was left but the chief. He raced to the sea. He swam far out to sea. Lava rocks followed him. Ocean waters put out the fires of Pele.

The chief was not caught, but everyone else was. There, near Kapoho in Puna, you may see the rough lava flow which, the story says, covered all the people on the day of the holua race.

THE STONES OF KANE

Long, long ago, two brothers and their sister came through the waters of the ocean toward Kauai. They had the form of stones.

They came near Haena Bay. The sister said, "Let us stay here."

Her brothers said to her, "If you stay here, seaweed will cover you. Shell fish will stick to you. People will walk over you when they go fishing."

The sister said, "If you go on to the mountains, birds will light on you. Lizards will crawl over you. Let us stay here."

The brothers went on to the shore. The sister stayed in Haena Bay. She is there today. You can see her at low tide. Seaweed has covered her. Shell fish have stuck to her. People have walked over her when they went fishing.

One brother was very tired. He went a little way from shore, and lay down to rest. "I shall stay here," he said. He is there today, covered with moss. His name is Pohaku-loa, or the Long Stone.

The second brother went on. He went on and on. He began to climb up the steep mountain slopes. He was very tired. He thought he could go no farther.

The god Kane saw him there, holding to the mountain. He was sorry for the traveler. He lifted him, and set him high on the mountain, on the edge of the ridge. You can see him there today. His name is Pohaku-o-Kane, or Stone of Kane.

APPENDIX C

Pronouncing Hawaiian Words

THE *vowels* of the Hawaiian language are a, e, i, o, u. The other letters are called *consonants*.

In Hawaiian, the vowels have these sounds:

> a, ah, as in father.
> e, ay as in bay; sometimes as e in met.
> i, ee as in see; sometimes as i in hill.
> o, as in hope.
> u, oo as in moon.

If you look up any word in your dictionary, you will find that it is divided into parts. Each part is a syllable. In the Hawaiian language, every syllable always ends with a vowel. This makes a difference in the pronunciation. For example, the word Honolulu is divided this way: Ho-no-lu-lu. It is pronounced the way it is divided. The first syllable is Ho, never hon.

In the Hawaiian language, every vowel should be pronounced. Sometimes the separate sounds are made quickly, so quickly that you can hardly hear the separate vowel sounds. The ai sound is an example of this. The ah-ee, said quickly, sounds almost

184

like i in light. This happens when the two vowels are said smoothly, as in the word Kailua.

Sometimes two vowels, coming together, are not spoken smoothly. There is a sharp break between them. In this pronunciation list, the break is shown by an upside-down comma. Wherever you see this, think the k sound, but do not say it. There was once a k in such words, but it has been dropped.

An example of this is Molokai, pronounced Mo-lo-ka'ee, with the accent on the ka, and a rough break between the ah and ee sounds.

Many Hawaiian words have more than one accented syllable. The apostrophe shows where the accents come. For example, we show the pronunciation of Kamehameha this way: Ka-may'-ha-may'-ha.

HAWAIIAN NAMES AND WORDS USED IN THIS BOOK

ahakea (a-ha-kay'-a) a tree

ahi (a'-hee) a fish

Aiai (A'-ee'a'-ee) the hero of an old story

aku (a'-ku) a fish

Alae (A'-la-e) land section, Hawaii

alae (a-la'-e) a bird

alahee (a-la-hay'ay) a tree

amaama (a'-ma-a'-ma) a fish

Anahola (A'-na-ho'-la) land section, Kauai

Anuenue (A-nu'-e-nu'-e) hill, Hawaii

ape (a'-pe) a plant

auwai (a'-u-wa'-ee) an irrigation ditch

elepaio (e'lepa'-i-o) a bird

Ewa (E'-va) district, Oahu

haa (ha-a') a tree

Haena (Ha'-e'-na) valley, Kauai

Hakea (Ha-kay'-a) name given to the bow of a canoe. It comes from *ahakea*, the wood often used for the rim.

hala (ha'-la) a tree

Halai (Ha-la'i) hill, Hilo

Halawa (Ha-la'-wa) valley, Molokai

Haleakala (Ha'-lay-a'-ka-la') mountain, Maui

Halepo (Ha'-lay'-po). A name given to a surf board. Means *earth-colored*. The Hawaiians often named favorite surf boards, calabashes, poi bowls, and other possessions. *Halepo* was probably a beautiful brown board.

Hamakua (Ha'-ma-ku'-a) district, Hawaii

Hanalei (Ha'-na-lay'-ee) valley, Kauai

hau (ha'-u) a tree

Hawaii (Ha-wa'-ee'ee) an island

Hawaii-loa (Ha-wa'-ee'ee lo'-a) man's name

Heeia (He'-e-i'-a) place, Oahu

Hilo (Hee'-lo) district, Hawaii

Hina (Hee'-na) Maui's mother

hinalea (hee'-na-lay'-a) a fish

holei (ho'-le-i) a fish

holua (ho'-lu'-a) a sled

Honolulu (Ho'-no-lu'-lu) place, Oahu

Hualalai (Hu'-a-la-la'-ee) mountain, Hawaii

huki (hu'-ki) to pull

hukilau (hu'-ki-la'-u) a way of fishing

ieie (i'-e-i'-e) a vine

Ieie (I'-e-i'-e) channel between Kauai and Oahu

iiwi (i'ee-wii) a bird

ilima (i-lee'-ma) a flower

imu (ee'-mu) an oven

Iwa (Ee'-wa) character in an old story

Kaaawa (Ka-a-a'-wa) valley, Oahu

Kaala (Ka-a'-la) mountain, Oahu

Kaena (Ka'-e'-na) headland, Oahu

Kahaloa (Ka'-ha-lo'-a) land section, Oahu

Kahana (Ka-ha'-na) valley, Oahu

Kahoolawe (Ka-ho'o-la'-ve) an island

Kahului (Ka-hu'-lu'-i) place, Maui

Kailua (Ka'-ee-lu'-a) bay, Hawaii; many other places have this name

Ka-imu-kalua-ua (Ka-ee'-mu-ka-lu'-a-u'-a) temple, Molokai

kala (ka'-la) a fish

Kalia (Ka-lee'-a) land section, Oahu

kamani (ka-ma'-ni) a tree

Kamehameha (Ka-may'-ha-may'-ha) the first king of all the islands

Kanaloa (Ka'-na-lo'-a) a god

Kane (Ka'-ne) a god

Kaneohe (Ka'-ne-o'-he) bay, Oahu

kapa (ka'pa) bark cloth

Kapalilua (Ka-pa'-li-lu'-a) land section, Hawaii

Kapo (Ka'po) a goddess

Kapoho (Ka'-po'-ho) land section, Hawaii

Kapoi (Ka'po'-i) character in an old story

kapu (ka'-pu) forbidden

Kapunohu (Ka-pu'-no-hu') character in an old story

Kau (Ka-u') district, Hawaii

Kauai (Ka'-u-a'ee) an island

kauila (ka'-u-ee'-la) a tree

Kawaihae (Ka-wa'-ee-ha'-e) bay, Hawaii

Kawaipuolo (Ka-wa'-ee-pu'o-lo) spring, Waialua

kawau (ka'-wa'u) a tree

Kawelo (Ka-way'-lo) a chief

Keaau (Kay'-a-a'u) village, Puna. Also character in an old story

Kealakekua (Ke-a'-la-ke-ku'-a) bay, Hawaii

Kealia (Kay'-a-lee'-a) place, Kauai

Kewalo (Kay-wa'-lo) land section, Oahu

kihei (kee'-hay'-i) a shawl

Kiholo (Ki-ho'-lo) bay, Hawaii

Kikiaola (Ki'ki'-a-o'-la) Ola's water way

Kilauea (Kee-la'-u-ay'-a) volcano, Hawaii

koa (ko'-a) a tree

Kohala (Ko-ha'-la) district, Hawaii, mountains, Hawaii

Koloa (Ko'-lo'-a) land section, Kauai

Kolopule (Ko'-lo-pu'-le) stream, Hawaii

Koolau (Ko'o-la'-u) windward districts; mountain range, Oahu

Kona (Ko'-na) district, Hawaii

kou (ko'-u) a tree

Ku (Ku') a god

Kualoa (Ku'-a-lo'-a) land section, Oahu

kukui (ku'-ku'-ee) a tree

Kuula (Ku'u-la) character in an old story

Laakona (La'a-ko'-na) a chief of Ewa

Laka (La'-ka) character in an old story

Lanai (La'-na'i) an island

lau (la'-u) leaf

lauhala (la'-u-ha'-la) leaf of the hala

Lawai (La'-wa'i) land section, Kauai

lehua (lay'-hu'-a) a flower

lei (lay'-ee) wreath

Lonokaeho (Lo'-no-ka-e'-ho) a chief

Maalaea (Ma'a-la'-e-a) bay, Maui

maile (ma'-i-le) a vine

Makahiki (Ma'-ka-hi'-ki) a season of the year

makaloa (ma'-ka'-lo'-a) a plant

Makapuu (Ma'-ka-'pu'u) headland, Oahu

Makuakeke (Ma-ku'-a-ke'-ke) a chief

Makupane (Ma'ku-pa'-ne) point, Hawaii

malo (ma′-lo) man's clothing

mamaki (ma′-ma′-kee) a plant

mamane (ma′-ma′-ne) a tree

mamo (ma-mo′) a bird

Manoa (Ma-no′-a) valley, Oahu

Maui (Ma′-u-i) an island

Mauna Kea (Ma′-u-na Kay′-a) mountain, Hawaii

Mauna Loa (Ma′-u-na Lo′-a) mountain, Ha-Hawaii

menehune (may′-ne-hu′-ne) the little men in the old stories

milo(mee′-lo) a tree

Mokapu (Mo-ka′-pu) point, Oahu

mokihana (mo′-ki-ha′-na) a tree

Molokai (Mo′-lo-ka'ee) an island

Moo Kuna (Mo′o Ku′-na) island, Wailuku River, Hilo

Naalehu (Na'a-lay′-hu) place, Hawaii

naio (na′-ee-o) a tree

Nawiliwili (Na-wi′-li-wi′-li) land section, Kauai

nau (na′-u) a plant

Niihau (Ni'i-ha′-u) an island

noni (no′-ni) a tree

Nuuanu (Nu'u-a′-nu) valley, Oahu

Oahu (O-a′-hu) an island

ohia ai (o-hi'a a′-ee) a tree

ohia ha (o-hi'a ha′) a tree

ohia lehua (o-hi'a lay′-hu′-a) a tree

Ola (O′-la) character in an old story

olapa (o-la′-pa) a tree

olona (o′-lo-na′) a plant

oo (o'o) a bird

o-o (o-o′) digging stick

opihi (o-pee′-hee) a small fish

Paao (Pa′-a′-o) a chief

paiai (pa'i-a'i) pounded taro

Panaewa (Pa′-na-e′-wa) forest, Hawaii

pau (pa-u′) woman's dress

Pele (Pay'-le) a goddess

pili (pee'-li) a grass

Pohaku-loa (Po-ha'-ku-lo'a) stone, Kauai

Pohaku-o-Kane (po-ha'-ku-o-Ka'-ne) stone, Kauai

pohuehue (po'-hu'-e-hu'-e) a vine

poi (po'-ee) food made from taro

Puna (Pu'-na) district, Hawaii

Puuloa (Pu'u-lo'-a) land section, Oahu

ti (tee) a plant

uhu (u'-hu) a fish

uki (u'-ki) a plant

Umi (U'-mee) a King of Hawaii

Wahiawa (Wa'-hi-a-wa') place, Oahu

Waiakea (Wa'-ee-a-kay-a) land section, Hawaii

Waialeale (Wa'-ee-a'-le-a'-le) mountain, Kauai

Waialua (Wa'-ee-a-lu'-a) place, Oahu

Waianae (Wa'-ee-a-na'-e) land section, Oahu; mountain range, Oahu

Waiau (Wa'-ee-a'-u) stream, Hilo

Wailua (Wa'-ee-lu'-a) stream, Kauai

Wailuku (Wa'-ee-lu'-ku) stream, Hilo. Name given to other places.

Waimea (Wa'-ee-may'-a) bay, Kauai. Name given to many other places in the Islands.

Waipio (We'-ee-pee'-o) valley, Hawaii. Name given to other places.

wauke (wa'-u-ke) a plant

wiliwili (wi'-li-wi'-li) a tree

Index